THE
BLUE GRASS
COOK BOOK

"THE TURBANED MISTRESS OF A
KENTUCKY KITCHEN"

THE
BLUE GRASS
COOK BOOK

Compiled by
MINNIE C. FOX

With an Introduction by
JOHN FOX JR.

New Introduction by
TONI TIPTON-MARTIN

THE UNIVERSITY PRESS OF KENTUCKY

Published in 2005 by the University Press of Kentucky
First edition published in 1904
New introduction copyright © 2005 by The University Press of Kentucky
Paperback edition 2012

Scholarly publisher for the Commonwealth,
serving Bellarmine University, Berea College, Centre College of Kentucky,
Eastern Kentucky University, The Filson Historical Society, Georgetown
College, Kentucky Historical Society, Kentucky State University, Morehead
State University, Murray State University, Northern Kentucky University,
Transylvania University, University of Kentucky, University of Louisville,
and Western Kentucky University.
All rights reserved.

Editorial and Sales Offices: The University Press of Kentucky
663 South Limestone Street, Lexington, Kentucky 40508-4008
www.kentuckypress.com

16 15 14 13 12   5 4 3 2 1

Illustrations by A. L. Coburn, from the original edition

Library of Congress Cataloging-in-Publication Data

Fox, Minnie C.
  The blue grass cook book / compiled by Minnie C. Fox ; with an intro-
duction by John Fox Jr. ; new introduction by Toni Tipton-Martin.
     p. cm.
  Originally published: New York : Fox, Duffield & Co., 1904.
  ISBN-13: 978-0-8131-2381-3 (hardcover : alk. paper)
  ISBN-10: 0-8131-2381-X (hardcover : alk. paper) 1. Cookery, American—
Southern style. 2. Cookery—Kentucky. I. Tipton-Martin, Toni. II. Title.
  TX715.2.S68F69 2005
  641.5975—dc22   2005028430
  ISBN 978-0-8131-4112-1 (pbk. : alk. paper)

This book is printed on acid-free paper meeting the requirements of
the American National Standard for Permanence in Paper for Printed
Library Materials.

Manufactured in the United States of America.

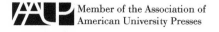 Member of the Association of
American University Presses

Bluegrass and Black Magic

An Introduction to the New Edition

Toni Tipton-Martin

The written word has been cruel to African American cooks, and that truth alone makes the unearthing and reproduction of *The Blue Grass Cook Book* a cause for celebration. Without even getting to the meat of the matter (or the bread, vegetables, desserts, and drinks), it is satisfying to give credit where it has long been due. This book, written by native Kentuckian Minnie C. Fox and first published in 1904, provides an honest and revealing picture of the state of culinary affairs in the South at the start of the twentieth century, and as such it accomplishes several wonderful things for modern-day readers.

First, it is a salutary redress to the African American descendants of generations of invisible cooks. It is also a long-delayed memorial to the white Southerners who loved and esteemed these hard-working and skillful women (and men) when it was not advisable or even socially acceptable to do so. And perhaps most important, this new facsimile edition of *The Blue Grass Cook Book* brings home to all a self-evident but seldom-expressed revelation: buried in the way things are lies a hidden truth about the way things used to be.

Generally speaking, historians have shown little interest in the state of domestic relations in the shaping of early American culture, and they have paid only minimal attention to the contributions of African American women. Were it not for the scholarship of such writers as Deborah Gray White, Jacqueline Jones, Susan Tucker, and a few others, we would have precious little to measure against the racist and sexist stereotypes of nineteenth-century Southern literature, with its repetitious assortment of scheming Jezebels, cantankerous Mammies, delicate Miss Charlottes, and grinning Aunt Jemimas. Apparently, the Fox family of Kentucky respected the true contributions of the women in their households.

The Blue Grass Cook Book is a clear and concise collection of more than three hundred recipes, plus a dozen stunning camera portraits of African American cooks at work. The book seems broadly representative of the culinary experiences of well-to-do white people in Kentucky a century ago. And the poignant (albeit time-bound) introduction written by Minnie's brother, the noted Kentucky novelist John Fox Jr., makes this volume a particularly valuable artifact for deeper exploration of the symbiotic relationship between black and white women in long-ago Southern kitchens.

More directly than anyone before them—or after, until midcentury—the Foxes publicly acknowledged the magnitude of the black contribution to Southern foodways, Southern culture, and Southern hospitality. In what amounts to direct and explicit homage, Minnie applauds the "turbaned mistress of the kitchen" for her dignity, wisdom, and talent. John Fox's introduction and the photographs by Alvin Langdon Coburn do for these great cooks what historians, cookbook authors, novelists, advertisers, and manufacturers simply did not: they single out for full recognition and credit the black cook as the near-invisible but indispensable figure who made Kentucky cuisine famous throughout the South and beyond.

Curiously, *The Blue Grass Cook Book* seems to have had a short life in the marketplace. Though it was published in New York, was introduced by a respected novelist, contained portraits by a photographer with international credentials, and was filled with classic recipes from black cooks and white matrons of the South, the book was never widely circulated. Newspapers of the time ignored it, and even when Minnie Fox died almost sixty years later, her published obituaries made no mention of the book; neither is there any reference to it in biographies of John Fox Jr. and the photographer A. L. Coburn. Now *The Blue Grass Cook Book* has languished in obscurity for fully a century, and the only proof that it ever existed at all is offered by the few copies still to be found in the stacks of some libraries.

Minnie Fox and her gallery of great Southern cooks came to my attention while I was trying to assemble the pieces of the African American female cook's scattered and incomplete history. In *Southern Food: At Home, on the Road, in History* (1987), John Egerton gave *The Blue Grass Cook Book* one of the few reviews it ever received (though he incorrectly identified Minnie Fox as John Fox's mother, not his sister). Egerton's exhaustive chronicle of Southern foodways was one of the earliest books to single out the contributions of

African American cooks to Southern cuisine. He writes: "In the most desolate and hopeless of circumstances, blacks caught in the grip of slavery often exhibited uncommon wisdom, beauty, strength, and creativity. The kitchen was one of the few places where their imagination and skill could have free rein and full expression, and there they often excelled. From the elegant breads and meats and sweets of plantation cookery to the inventive genius of Creole cuisine, from beaten biscuits to bouillabaisse, their legacy of culinary excellence is all the more impressive, considering the extremely adverse conditions under which it was compiled."

Elizabeth Fox-Genovese and other scholars of nineteenth-century American culture tell us that the collective story of African American women working in kitchens also calls attention to the plight of white women in that culture. Together they yielded to the demands of a male-dominated society—and together they also wielded a domestic power that neither could command separately. Their close and interdependent working relationship was most visible and significant in the upper South. In glimpsing the post–Civil War world inhabited by white mistresses like Minnie Fox and black cooks like "Aunt Dinah," we can better appreciate the rich culinary legacy created when two cultures came together over skillets of pone and pots of greens to evolve a historically important and still beloved cuisine.

Minerva Carr Fox's family roots in Kentucky trace back to 1795, just three years after statehood, when her Fox ancestors arrived from Virginia via the Wilderness Road. They settled on a plot of open land at a place called Stony Point in Bourbon County, about eight miles south of the new town of Paris, and for the next sixty years they grew prosperous educating the children in their community. As slavery was approaching its fiery demise in the 1850s, the landed gentry of Bourbon County, who prided themselves on their "idyllic" race relations, hoped to stay above the fray, but they were soon to be caught up in the rebellion that not only brought an end to slavery but also divided white Kentuckians into two irreconcilable camps.

It was in the parted wake of the Civil War that Minerva, one of ten children, was born in 1868, as the bracing reality of emancipation was sinking in for both black and white Southerners. Her father, John Fox Sr., a teacher, delivered classical instruction to white children in their corner of Bourbon County, and he showed sympathy for the plight of black families, to whom freedom had brought more uncertainty than opportunity. The elder Fox admired the former abolitionists who were becoming philanthropists, and he wanted the Freedman's Bureau to succeed in developing self-help organizations and institutions to steer newly liberated blacks toward full citizenship—by all accounts a slow and painful process, punctuated by diehard white resistance. Chaos and confusion still gripped postwar Kentucky, and hostility to change was especially acute in plantation counties like Bourbon, where the largest numbers of black residents were concentrated.

Little Minnie Fox flourished in the protective balm of her youth, oblivious to the wrenching changes taking place all around her. She was almost nine when Reconstruction ended in 1877. It was an ugly time in the South, a period defined by white determination to reassert authority over blacks and to view them, in the words of the historian Marion B. Lucas, as "social and economic enemies who did not deserve equal protection of the law." Minnie, together with her eight brothers and her sister, Elizabeth, attended both First Christian Church of Paris and their father's school regularly; they otherwise spent their leisure time in tranquil communion with nature and the arts. Theirs, she would recall later, was "a world of green grass dotted with dandelions and sweet with the fragrance of [blooming] locust [trees]." People of African descent were all around them, suffering their chronic status of inequality in silence.

From the earliest days of pioneer settlement, white farmers in the Bluegrass had expressed a wide range of attitudes toward the blacks under their control—from resentment and antipathy to tolerance and compassion. These sentiments found extreme expression in the years of uncertainty after the war. Some landowners in the commonwealth had been outspoken in their opposition to slavery, but the "peculiar institution" thrived in the rich Bluegrass soil nonetheless, and whether it was unremittingly harsh or more benignly paternalistic, it had dominated the region's economy. By far the most slaves thereabouts were concentrated on the large tobacco and hemp plantations in a fifty-mile radius of Lexington. Still, even in the heart of this area, Bourbon County included, some families of the landed gentry did not rely on slave labor. Minnie Fox's was one such family. Her great-grandfather William, her grandfather Boaz, and her father, John W. Fox Sr., all were educators in Clark County.

In what was received as a bitter irony by Kentucky abolitionists, Harriet Beecher Stowe set her 1852 antislavery novel, *Uncle Tom's Cabin*, in the heart of the Bluegrass, and she used the regional ambivalence toward bondage to frame an environment in which cruelty and inhumanity festered. Scholars have tirelessly debated whether slavery truly was more benign in the upper South than in the heart of Dixie; but in any case, the extended family of Minnie Fox was more or less identifiable within Stowe's cast of characters: Minnie's maternal antecedents, the Carrs of Virginia, were Confederates, while the Kentucky Foxes favored preserving the Union. The divided heart of this soon-to-be border state in the Civil War was fittingly framed in the near-simultaneous publication of Stowe's incendiary book and of a powerfully nostalgic song, "My Old Kentucky Home," written by the famed Kentucky composer Stephen Collins Foster.

In the passionately intense spirit of the abolitionists, Harriet Stowe sought to arouse hearts and minds against the brutality of slavery. With lyricism and sentimentality, Stephen Foster just as intently tried to soften slavery's image to one of innocence and benevolence. The message of his song, he once told an interviewer, was that "no matter how far we travel away from home, our hearts ache for the best memories of childhood, the security of family, and the familiarity of home." Two more diametrically opposed visions could hardly be imagined, and both would have tremendous staying power.

The graphic realism of *Uncle Tom's Cabin* spoke—and still speaks—for itself. "My Old Kentucky Home" found immortality too. It was a near-sacred hymn for ex-Confederate soldiers. Minstrel performers distorted it into a lament of former slaves for the security of the old plantation. The distinguished black composer Harry T. Burleigh and his mentor, Antonín Dvorák, further clouded its meaning by treating it as a "heart song" of the American people, an all-embracing folk song comparable to Negro spirituals. In the early 1900s W. E. B. DuBois gave his imprimatur to the song as "a legitimately authentic" anthem of the Negro race. Civil rights activists later challenged Foster's work for its "negative ethnic images." And to this day, "My Old Kentucky Home" (with its lyrics properly sanitized for the

sake of political correctness) retains its popularity
as the official state song.

Considering all the powerfully contradictory
emotional forces of antebellum times—forces that
survived the war itself, and Reconstruction, and
generations of "separate but equal" mythology—
one could easily forget that Minnie Fox's family
existed in a community and a region where former
slaves and their descendants continued to provide
personal services and domestic labor for multitudes
of white families, large and small, rich and middle
class. As freedmen and freedwomen, these labor-
ers relieved many a Bluegrass family of the oner-
ous chores of housekeeping and spared young
children like Minnie Fox the unrelenting hard work
associated with family life in her time. In general,
when all was said and done, black women continued to hold, deep into the twentieth century, the
same jobs they had performed as slaves—working
as cooks, nannies, washerwomen, domestic servants. The only difference was that they received a
little bit of money for their efforts.

Relatives, friends, and neighbors in and around
Paris remembered John Fox Sr. as a family man, a

naturalist, and a gifted teacher. His Stony Point Academy preceded public schools in the region by almost half a century, and its rigorous curriculum included Latin and Greek, mathematics, bookkeeping, and surveying. Ever the diligent headmaster, he left a vast catalog of his botanical research and a written record of his students' names, their achievements, and even their participation in the school's maintenance. Absent from his papers were any ledgers, journals, diaries, or sales receipts to indicate that he ever owned slaves.

In a compilation of letters and clippings about her novelist brother John, Elizabeth Fox described the enduring love that both her father and brother held for humanity and nature. In their independence and self-sufficiency, she wrote, they followed in the footsteps of Kentucky's pioneer founders. Though tobacco growers and whiskey makers dominated the local economy, none of the Fox men smoked or drank, she declared, and none "could bear the sight of suffering or evidence of the slightest pain in others." Elizabeth praised her father for "the fine example of a hard-working, upright life" grounded in religious training, which she said enriched their lives. He was a stern taskmaster, sometimes keeping his children up past midnight reciting their lessons. Reminiscing about their childhood years later, Minnie wrote in 1919 in her brother John's obituary: "There was kindness and hospitality there, but nothing light or frivolous. We were all grown before wine or cards were allowed in the house. Prayers in the morning and again at night; grace at meals, and the school always opened with Bible reading and prayer."

The picture of the Fox family that emerges is one of basic decency and benevolence in the context of a society in which, before and after slavery, white supremacy was a foregone conclusion. Even the most charitable of the privileged—and the Foxes were certainly that—accepted without question the view that blacks were their social and intellectual inferiors. When he wrote the introduction to his sister's cookbook forty years after the war, John Fox Jr. could still wax nostalgic about "the social system of the South [that] rested on the slave," under the guidance of "the [white] overseer, the black mammy and Aunt Dinah, the cook." It is hardly surprising, given the social and political atmosphere of resurgent racism in that time, that the younger John Fox and his white contemporaries, including Stephen Foster and James Lane

Allen, another Kentucky writer of note, would be caught up in the common lament for the "Lost Cause," which numerous historians have characterized as a genteel, self-satisfied culture made harmonious by benevolent masters whose creativity and productivity flourished with the faithful service of contented slaves.

In such a climate it was exceedingly rare for men or women of the majority race to acknowledge any debt to their "colored" or "Negro" servants, whether their African heritage was full-blooded or partial. Cookbooks originating from the South clearly reflected this; they had from the first and would continue to until well past the mid-1900s. (For that matter, practically all American cookbooks undervalued the contributions of black cooks, if they mentioned them at all.) As the cookbooks tell it, the antebellum plantation mistress would acquire a new recipe, read it to her kitchen slave, and then stand over her while she prepared the dish. The cook might later apply some African technique, or add a local ingredient, or incorporate a leftover into it, so that over time the dish would become something new and original, a "Southern creation," and the white mistress would take credit for it in the family recipe book and in collections of these "family heirlooms" passed from one generation to the next.

One such collection, coincidentally, was *Housekeeping in the Blue Grass*, published right there in Bourbon County by the ladies of the Paris Presbyterian Church in 1875. Minnie Fox was seven at the time, and she no doubt was thoroughly familiar with the book long before she compiled her own in 1904. In its preface *Housekeeping in the Blue Grass* did make an oblique reference to the fact that "many of our recipes are entirely original with our own famed cooks"—but even in that declarative remark, the possessive pronoun made clear who owned the dish (and, in effect, the cook too).

When "entirely original" recipes appear in the pages of Reconstruction-era community cookbooks, the black cook's contribution is routinely eclipsed. Aunt Dinah goes down in history as the provider of labor, not of ingenuity or originality. Dishes with African roots that passed from the slave cabin to the Big House often go on from the white family's kitchen to the cookbook and into culinary history. The African American cooks of the South and beyond were there from the start, shaping much of the culinary heritage of the region, but they were marginalized, and their contributions were largely ignored.

Surprisingly, Minnie Fox's *Blue Grass Cook Book* takes a different tack. The "turbaned mistress" so revered by John Fox Jr. in his introduction is not a literary construct, not an illiterate Mammy lifted from the pages of a moonlight-and-magnolias romance novel of the Old South. Rather, she is the kitchen genius, the culinary heroine, the great nurturer of soul and spirit. Far from simply stirring the pots and serving the food, she is a person whose food and wisdom have elevated the character of generations of Kentuckians. She is, says Fox, a woman worth going to battle for. "Is there a Southerner who does not hold her . . . in loving remembrance?" he declares, yet "as far as I know she has never got her just due."

All the Fox siblings grew up knowing the Aunt Dinahs of Bourbon County as well as they knew the parents of their contemporaries in Paris and beyond. As teenagers they saw these skilled black women perform the duties of surrogate mother in such grand homes as Auvergne, the palatial estate of Brutus and Anna Maria Clay, where Coburn took most of the photographs that appear in *The Blue Grass Cook Book.*

INTRODUCTION TO THE NEW EDITION

When Brutus Clay (whose brother, by the way, was the fiery abolitionist Cassius Marcellus Clay) built Auvergne with the help of 130 slaves in the 1840s, it was the largest plantation in Bourbon County, an agricultural and commercial enterprise that produced an abundance of livestock and row crops. Amelia Clay, the master's first wife, supervised the domestic activities of the slave women, which included spinning, weaving, sewing, gardening, and preserving enough to supply the resident family and their slaves. This managerial role eventually was conveyed to Brutus's second wife, Anna Maria, and it was she who directed the house servants who stayed on at Auvergne after emancipation.

Tangled within the braid of documentation now preserved at Auvergne by Brutus Clay's great-grandson Berle Clay are letters and photographs that help reconstruct the lives of some of the black families there who were the subjects of Coburn's portraits. "Aunt Frances" (opposite page 64) was the cheery wife of Hampton Ayers, who was born on the estate (as were three of his brothers, David, Israel, and Andrew, all of whom enlisted in the Union Army). George Brent (opposite page 98), photographed curing hams at Auvergne, was the son of "Aunt

Mahala," the Clay family cook between 1880 and 1900, when Minnie Fox was blossoming from an adolescent into a young woman.

Berle Clay's sister, Mary Clay, in a book called *Voices from the Century Before,* described George Brent as her "grandmother's general factotum," a man who could do anything and everything. Her brother Berle has his own remembrance, not unlike that symbolized by the classic cook-mistress relationship of old: "Grandmother and George were like right hand and left hand." George's name, he recalls, "was the last thing she said before she died."

It was bonds like these, not the bonds of slavery, that Minnie Fox came of age comprehending and that she would seek to honor in *The Blue Grass Cook Book,* which she produced when she was thirty-six years old, unmarried, and still living at home with her parents. In the interim, though, some major changes had come into the lives of the Fox family. First, two of her brothers, James and Horace, moved east into the mountains of Appalachia, where the railroads were opening the coalfields to mining, and there they became brokers speculating in the buying and selling of land. In the late 1880s, their home at Stony Point burned to the ground, and everything in it was destroyed. Then, in 1890, John Fox Sr., having retired from his mission as a schoolmaster, decided to relocate with his wife and some of their children—including Minnie—from the gently rolling Bluegrass hills of Bourbon County to the craggy coal-country town of Big Stone Gap, Virginia, near where the Fox brothers (including John, Jr., an 1883 graduate of Harvard) were seeking their fortunes. It was to be the Fox family's last home, and it was from there that Minnie would look back in longing to her old Kentucky home as she completed her cookbook in 1904.

From all appearances, life was harder for the Foxes in those years than it had been in Bourbon County. Big Stone Gap lacked the grace and charm of Paris—and, there being no history of a plantation economy on those steep and rocky slopes, there were virtually no black families nearby with skilled cooks and servants for hire. Further, the work was not only hard (coal mining and timber cutting) but risky, and the Fox men were as susceptible as everyone else to the boom-and-bust rhythms of such extractive industries. John Fox Jr. briefly took up pick and shovel with his brothers to build an access road to enhance the value of their coal-rich acreage, but he soon decided that writing novels was a more appealing vocation. His novels and short stories began pouring forth in 1895, bringing him wide renown. (Prominent New York houses published all fourteen of his books, tales of romance and adventure woven in the rich texture of the mountains, notably *The Little Shepherd of Kingdom Come* and *The Trail of the Lonesome Pine.*) The books also landed him prestigious assignments as a war correspondent in Cuba and the Orient.

It was during one such adventure, in Japan, that John received a letter from Minnie asking him to write the introduction to her recipe collection. He was six years older than she, a big brother whose maturity and discipline she had always admired, and whose success as a writer she envied. He had always encouraged her, too. One of his undated letters to Minnie bore this advice: "I think you've got a genuine talent and all you've got to do is work, work, work. Write simply and sincerely. Simplicity and sincerity and strength, then originality and distinction, that's the course for you. Study everybody, imitate nobody. Be yourself always." She knew he shared her admiration for the black cooks of their youth, and for the Bluegrass; he was the perfect person, in her view, to introduce the sweet tale of the cooks, their food, and the land for which the Foxes never ceased to long.

In life and work, Minnie Fox was the centrist in a polarized community. By the time she finished amassing recipes for *The Blue Grass Cook Book*, the nation was in the throes of an entirely restructured social order. Black servants fled the hard and thankless work in Southern households for better job opportunities in the promised land of the North. The housewife received a new mantle of dignity as domestic duties moved away from the dark, dim realm of arduous—and frequently demeaning—household chores into the light of science and art. Cookbooks appeared in record numbers, and most of them appealed in one way or another to the emotional needs of frustrated housewives who had lost their helpmates. These tomes were the salve that soothed sore Southern egos.

At one end of this publishing bonanza were wistful plantation-style cookbooks that mingled "fine old Dixie dishes" with demoralizing etchings of slaves at work, vernacular language, and lyrics from spirituals and hymns—collections designed to spur on young housekeepers who had very little experience and virtually no kitchen help. The remainder of this spate of household manuals emphasized domestic economy and food science; included were such culinary endeavors as Jennie C. Benedict's *Blue Ribbon Cook Book,* which was published by the editor of the *Louisville Courier-Journal*'s Household Department in the same year that *The Blue Grass Cook Book* appeared on the market. *The Blue Ribbon Cook Book*'s "tested" recipes served as a reminder to neophyte housewives that cooking "possesses the dignity of an art, of science, and of philosophy." The popular little text also encouraged them to "get rid of the false sentiment that grades different ranks of work as more or less respectable."

In between, there was Miss Minnie, known among the circle of elite hostesses in Paris and Big Stone Gap for the rich tapestry of her hospitality. She threw remarkable parties for John Fox, appealing to the sophisticated palates and cosmopolitan tastes of his publishing-world friends with "very fine," "excellent," and "particularly nice" chafing dish recipes, such as Coquilles of Chicken, Sweetbreads with Champignons, and the Italian sweet and sour sauce *Agrodolce* (misinterpreted by the cook as "Agra Dolce"). Contrasted against the ambitious drive of her contemporaries toward culinary mastery, Miss Minnie's culinary passion and her obvious breaks from the publishing norm—whether intentional or inadvertent—suggest a woman on a creative limb who penetrated insular post–Civil War Southern kitchens and uncloaked a quietly kept African American aphorism: the mistress may have determined the menu, selected the china, crystal, and linens, even set her own table, but when it came to the food, it was the black woman whose dishes breathed life into the party.

As *The Blue Grass Cook Book* regaled its audience with the delicacies enjoyed by Kentucky socialites, Miss Minnie's elegant recipe selection, though surprisingly delicious, neglected the needs of the growing population of desperate housewives in her midst. The cookbook was not about what to eat and how to cook it; it ignored basic kitchen wisdom, avoided common themes like stewed game and plain sauces, and shunned any mention of culinary alchemy or home remedies. Rather than detailed guidelines for kitchen novices, whose success demands precise cooking times, temperatures, and measurements, it tended to offer puzzlingly unspecific formulas. Bread bakers, for instance, were expected to have preexisting knowledge of how to "set a sponge as for white bread," or to know that egg whites must be beaten separately before being added to fritter batter. A further evidence of Miss Minnie's eclectic and often esoteric culinary approach, despite the formulaic trend, is her commingling—often on the same page—of old English kitchen measuring terms (kitchen spoons, dessert spoons, and teacups) with American standard measures (tablespoons, teaspoons, cups, pints, quarts).

The Blue Grass Cook Book updated the traditional block-recipe format, in which ingredients and instructions are combined into a single narrative, when it adopted the formula cookbook authors employ today (ingredients enumerated in a list that is followed by a narrative of the method). Unfortunately, the gloss of novelty turns dull when the formula is incompletely and inconsistently applied. Some recipes in the collection adhered to the new system, a few others reached back to time-honored tradition, and others still—Sally Lunn, for example—included both.

Nearly fifty members of the Kentucky and western Virginia aristocracy contributed recipes to Miss Minnie's collection, and at least half those women also had donated recipes to the Presbyterian Church ladies' *Housekeeping in the Blue Grass,* published nearly thirty years earlier. Except for differences in design—recipes in *Housekeeping in the Blue Grass* followed the block method—many of the recipes that appeared in both books, having passed between generations, were virtually the same. Curiously, the names of the contributors whose recipes appear in both collections are left out of *The Blue Grass Cook Book.* For example, Mrs. Henry C. Buckner offers her recipe for Cream Muffins in *Housekeeping:* "Take one and a half pints flour, whites only of two eggs; do not use yelks [*sic*] at all; a little salt, just enough sweet cream to make the batter right consistency. Grease muffin irons, have them hot, and pour them half full. Bake quickly." *The Blue Grass Cook Book*'s version of Cream Muffins (page 15) is certainly better organized, but it calls for the same amounts of liquid and dry ingredients, follows identical preparation instructions, even shares the same language—all without identifying the woman who submitted it. The same can be said for Hayden Salad, Oil Mangoes (which are not the now-familiar tropical fruit, but sweet bell peppers), and Baked Ham, among others. Miss Minnie did this perhaps to invigorate heirloom recipes, but the practice illustrates the paradox of early American kitchens: possession of a formula doesn't necessarily make one a thoughtful or competent cook.

Another attribution oddity involves the erratic identification of African American recipes. The culinary publishing industry has long presumed that changing a single ingredient or step in the method spawns a new dish and therefore new ownership. This standard allows that even a cook whose imagination is first stirred by a written recipe, but who substitutes key lime juice for lemon, opts for a different cut of meat, increases the amount of sweetening or for that matter changes sugar to molasses, can and should expect her name to follow the recipe's title. The habit of disregarding this rule when the cook was black is brought into clear view in *The Blue Grass Cook Book,* but ultimately the compilation raises more questions than it answers.

Black cooks are photographed preparing Mt. Airy Beaten Biscuits (page 1) and Kentucky Corn Dodgers (page 11), yet neither recipe is associated with the cook by title or tag line. Similarly, George Brent, the all-around handyman for the Clay family, is photographed curing ham at Auvergne, yet he is not credited with either of the two cured-ham recipes (nor is his name mentioned in the photo caption) in the meat section. Yet, Marcellus, who must have held a very special place at Auvergne and in the hearts the Paris community, is acknowledged over and again for his corn muffins and cornmeal batter cakes, for his wheat muffins, his omelet, his chocolate and peach ice creams, and his potato soups. Intentional snub? Perhaps, but we can be grateful that, coming as it did at the end of an era in American culinary history when generations of white Southerners took for granted that ownership of the black cook extended proprietary rights to her creations, *The Blue Grass Cook Book* offered some credit where previously there was none at all.

And so with all its innovations, *The Blue Grass Cook Book* made its appearance and then all too quickly slipped out of sight and mind. The reasons are still mystifying. Perhaps John Fox's words of praise for the black cooks were too candidly positive for those newly recharged segregationist times. Or maybe the white matrons who bought and read the lion's share of cookbooks were put off by the implication of a synergistic relationship between themselves and their black cooks—shown in words and pictures (not caricatures) to possess an air of egalitarian dignity. Whatever the case, this altogether selfless effort by Minnie C. Fox one hundred years ago is finally getting a second life, and for that we can be thankful. Its pioneering spirit, its matter-of-fact embrace of quality and equality—and, not least, its wonderfully representative Southern culinary classics—are enough to raise hope that present and future generations will peel away the lingering myths and stereotypes of the past and discover the hidden qualities of greatness in both races—and thereby restore to all cooks, of every race, those lean years the locusts ate.

Acknowledgments

The research and writings of scholars and historians too numerous to name have indeed tilled the soil that made way for a reprint of this groundbreaking book, and I thank them. But it is the members of the Fox and Clay families, the librarians, archivists, and various members of the Paris, Kentucky, and Big Stone Gap, Virginia, communities whose generosity showered me with resources, the unwritten obscurities and local oddities that breathed life into the work of Minnie C. Fox. Thank you, John Fox, Hermie Fox, Edward S. (Tim) Fox, Barbara Polly, Nancy Hobbs, Berle Clay, Jeff Bell, Thomas E. Stephens, Kenney Roseberry, John Egerton, John T. Edge, Ronni Lundy, and Dr. George C. Wright. I thank Joyce Harrison, my editor, for valuing this story and being my advocate at the University Press of Kentucky, and I also appreciate Trina Gibbins, Paul Barrett, and all the members of the International Association for Culinary Professionals' Harry A. Bell Grant Committee for their esteem and support of this project. I owe a tremendous debt to my friends and family, who nurtured and encouraged with words and deeds during creative drafts. To my husband, Bruce, and our children, Brandon, Jade, Christian, and Austin, I am particularly grateful; thank you for your loving patience and perseverance.

Introduction

IT is not wise for a man who can get sea-
sick in a rowboat on a mill-pond to
attack a Japanese dinner just after a seven-
teen days' voyage across the Pacific. I was
just that unwise, and for that reason perhaps
can do but scant justice in this Land of the
Rising Sun, to a soup in which floats bits of
strange fishes from the vasty deep, unknown
green things and an island of yellow custard;
to slices of many colored raw fish, tough
cocks' combs (real ones) or even to the
stewed chicken which at this dinner at least
had been shorn of everything except bones
and tough sinews. The other day I tried it
again with no better success, and now with
the prospect of rice for food three times a
day in the field around Port Arthur and no

bread (there can be no more serious depriva-
tion to a Southerner) I am suddenly asked
to think of a Kentucky table and that turbaned mistress of the Blue Grass kitchen, a
Kentucky cook!

It is June in Japan, and it is June in that
blessed land of the Blue Grass. The sun
shines there, no doubt, right now: the corn
top's ripe; the meadows are in bloom and
along turnpike and out in the fields the
song and laughter of darkies make gay the
air. It is early morning. The singing of
birds comes through the open windows—the
chatter of blackbirds and the mid-air calls of
far away meadow larks. Through those
windows sleepy eyes see wood and field,
with stretches of blossoming blue grass rippling in the wind. Another half-conscious
doze for an hour, another awakening, and by
your bed stands a black boy in a snowy
apron, his white teeth shining, and in his
kindly black paws a silver goblet on a silver
tray. Heavens, how it hurts to smell that
mint this far away! The goblet is gleaming
with frost, and the mint is still drenched

with dew. Who was it sang of the ecstasy of awakening on a June morning and being in love? Well, to the wise one who has that blissful state only as a memory a hint is sufficient.

It is now breakfast time. There are strawberries in Japan, but there are also strawberries in the Blue Grass, and I shall not risk international complications by invidious comparison. In the Blue Grass they go with a yellow cream of which I dare not think. You shall find that same cream in a cup of fragrant coffee as well. There is broiled ham with a grateful odor whose source is a mystery; there are plates of hot thin meal batter cakes, each encircled with crisp, delicate black embroidery, and there is golden butter that melts and drips and seeps between the layers. It is too early for game-birds, so those little brown, fat, broiled things resting in the big dish are spring chickens, "frying size," as we say in the Blue Grass, and on another dish there they are again—fried, after Southern style, half submerged in a rich cream of gravy, snow

white. I can go no further now, for the
waffles are yet to come.

You climb a horse now and ride out into
the morning and the sunlight and the fresh
air, into the singing of those birds and the
rippling stretches of blue grass, wheat and
barley and wind-shaken corn. Under full-
leafed maples and oaks and sycamores where
fat cattle are tearing up rich mouthfuls of
grass, and sheep and young lambs are graz-
ing and playing along a creek whose banks
are grassy to the very water's edge. Three
hours you ride, for you must see the whole
place that morning. Guests are coming to
dinner, and there will be little time in the
afternoon, so through lanes in which the
wild rose blooms and through woods and
meadows you lope for home. How hungry
you are ! The pike gate slams, the first
guest is coming, and up the hill they wind in
buggy, carriage, and on horseback. When
all are gathered in the drawing-room, you
shall see the host quietly lead some man to
the veranda—it is a magic signal that need
not be explained. Out there are more of

those frosted silver goblets, flowering with green and " with beaded bubbles winking at the brim."

And now dinner.

The dining-room is the biggest and sunniest in the house. On the wall are hunting prints, pictures of game and stag heads. The table runs almost the length of it, and the snowy table-cloth hangs almost to the floor. Before your hostess is a great tureen of calf's-head soup; before your host a saddle of venison, drenched in a bottle of ancient Madeira and flanked by flakes of red-currant jelly. Before one guest are broiled wild ducks. After the venison comes a great turkey, and last of all a Kentucky ham.

" That ham! Mellow, aged, boiled in champagne, baked brown, spiced deeply, rosy pink within and of a flavor and fragrance to shatter the fast of a pope; and without a brown-edged white layer so firm that the deft carving knife passing through gave no hint to the eye that it was delicious fat. . . . The rose flakes dropped under the knife in such thin slices that the edges coiled."

After the ham the table-cloth is lifted and the dessert spread on another lying beneath. Then that, too, is raised and the nuts and wines are placed on a third—red damask this time. So much for breakfast and dinner— the old-time dinner. At the thought of supper the pen of this exile halts, and for it the reader may search within.

Is it any wonder that the stories of Southern hospitality are so many and so good? It is said that in Texas a planter will sometimes waylay the passing stranger, and at the point of a shot-gun force him to halt and stay a month. I have heard of a man stopping to spend the night on a Georgia plantation and staying on for twenty years. I have heard of an old major in Virginia, the guest of the father of a friend of mine, who every spring had his horse saddled and brought to the fence, when the following annual colloquy took place:

"Oh, you'd better stay a while longer, Major," the host would say.

"No," the Major would say, " I reckon I'd better be goin'."

After every mint julep this interchange would take place. At the end of the third the Major invariably weakened.

" Well," he would say, "I reckon I'll stay a little longer." And he would stay—another year. This went on for a decade.

These things I have heard—what follows I know. There was a famous place near Lexington once which I will call Silver Springs, and there was a guest there of twenty years' standing. One morning he went over to the home of his host's son, liked it over there and stayed ten years until he died. But there is yet a better story of Silver Springs. So many guests actually died there that the host provided them with a graveyard. Some fifteen years ago the church near by was torn down, the graveyard was sold, and all the bodies had to be removed. The son of the master of Silver Springs wrote to what relatives of the dead guests he could find. No answer came, and the daughter of the son, who has been a lifelong friend of mine, took the seven guests, sang "Nearer, my God, to Thee" over them, and buried them in the family plot. There the seven rest to-day.

Now the social system of the South rested on the slave, and the three pillars of the substructure were the overseer, the black mammy and Aunt Dinah, the cook. But for Aunt Dinah would the master have had the heart for such hospitality? Would the guest have found it so hard to get away? Would stories like these ever have been born? Would the Kentuckian have had the brawn and brain that have given him such a history? Would Kentucky have sent the flower of her youth, forty thousand strong, into the Confederacy; would she have lifted the lid of her treasury to Lincoln, and in answer to his every call sent him a soldier practically without a bounty and without a draft; and when the curtain fell on the last act of the great tragedy would she have left half of her manhood behind it —helpless from disease, wounded or dead on the battlefield? I think not.

All honor then to that turbaned mistress of the Kentucky kitchen—the Kentucky cook. She came to the Blue Grass from Virginia more than a hundred years ago, swift on the flying feet of the Indian. She was broad, portly, kind of heart, though severe of countenance, as befitted her dignity, and usually quick of temper and sharp of tongue. Her realm was not limited to the kitchen. She disputed the power of "mammy" in the drawing-room, and there were times when all, black and white, bowed down before her. James Lane Allen has written that, going home with a friend late one night after a party, his friend got up at five o'clock the next morning and made him get up, through fear of rousing the temper of this same black, autocratic cook. But when she was kind she was mighty; and is there a Southerner who does not hold her, in spite of her faults, in loving remembrance? As far as I know she has never got her just due. She is gone, and there are good ones to-day who fill her place, but none who are full worthy. Publicly I acknowledge an everlasting debt, and to that turbaned mistress of the Kentucky kitchen gratefully this Southerner takes off his hat.

JOHN FOX, Jr.

TOKIO, JAPAN, June 1, 1904.

DEDICATED TO

Mrs. John B. Payne
Mrs. Henry C. Buckner
Mrs. William E. Simms
Mrs. John W. Fox

List of Contributors

ADDISON, MRS. WALTER E., . . Pulaski, Va.
ALEXANDER, MRS. A. J., . . Woodburn, Ky.
ALEXANDER, MISS KATE, . . Paris, Ky.
BASHFORD, MISS MARY, . . Paris, Ky.
BERRYMAN, MRS. CHARLES, . Lexington, Ky.
BERRYMAN, MRS. J. C., . . Lexington, Ky.
BRENT, MRS. C., ... Paris, Ky.
BUCKNER, MRS. HENRY C., . Paris, Ky.
BUCKNER, MRS. B. F., . . Paris, Ky.
BUCKNER, MRS. W. T., . . Winchester, Ky.
CABELL, MRS. C. ELLET, . . Berryville, Va.
CLAY, MRS. BRUTUS J., . . Bourbon Co., Ky.
CLAY, MRS. CASSIUS M., . . Paris, Ky.
CLAY, MRS. JAMES E., . . Paris, Ky.
COCHRAN, MRS. CAMPBELL
   CARRINGTON, ... Big Stone Gap, Va.
CROXTON, MISS VIRGINIA, . . Tappahannock, Va.
DABNEY, MISS, ... Bothwell, Va.
FITHIAN, MRS. WASH., . . Paris, Ky.
FOX, MRS. JOHN W., . . . Big Stone Gap, Va.
GARRARD, MRS., ... Bourbon Co., Ky.
GODDARD, MRS. MARY E., . Fleming Co., Ky.
GOFF, MRS. STRAUDER, . . Winchester, Ky.

GORTON, MRS. FRANCIS, . .	Rochester, N. Y.
HANSON, MRS. R. H., . .	Lexington, Ky.
HEDGES, MRS. JOHN T., . .	Paris, Ky.
HOLT, MRS. JOSEPH, . . .	Paris, Ky.
JOHNSON, MRS. W. A., . .	Paris, Ky.
LYLE, MISS ANNIE, . . .	Paris, Ky.
McCORMICK, MRS. CYRUS, .	Berryville, Va.
McCORMICK, MRS. FRANCIS, .	Berryville, Va.
McDOWELL, MRS. H. C., . .	Lynchburg, Va.
MASSIE, MRS. W. W., . .	Paris, Ky.
MOORE, MRS. A., ...	Berryville, Va.
NEELY, MRS. ROBERT J., . .	Paris, Ky.
PAYNE, MRS. JOHN B., . .	Lexington, Ky.
ROSSER, MRS. THOMAS L., .	Charlottesville, Va.
ST. NICHOLAS HOTEL, . . .	Cincinnati, Ohio.
SIMMS, MRS., ...	Paris, Ky.
SIMMS, MRS. WILLIAM E., .	Spring Station, Ky.
SPEARS, MRS. WOODFORD, .	Paris, Ky.
THORNTON, MRS. RICHARD, .	Lexington, Ky.
WEBB, MRS. MARY, . . .	Paris, Ky.
WENTZ, MRS. DANIEL B., .	Big Stone Gap, Va.
WHITE, MISS ANNIE, . . .	Abingdon, Va.
WHITE, MISS ELISE, . . .	Abingdon, Va.
WYLES, MRS. TOM R., . .	Chicago, Ill.

List of Illustrations

Contents

BREADS

li

EGGS

CONTENTS

SOUPS

CONTENTS

ENTRÉES

CROQUETTES

FOWL

GAME

CONTENTS

MEATS

SAUCES (FOR ENTRÉES, FISH, FOWL, AND MEATS)

CONTENTS

VEGETABLES

SALADS

CONTENTS

DRESSINGS FOR SALADS

ICE CREAM

ICES, PUNCHES, AND SHERBETS

CONTENTS

CREAMS AND OTHER DESSERTS

JELLIES

CONTENTS

SAUCES FOR PUDDINGS

CAKES

CONTENTS

FILLINGS FOR CAKES

BEVERAGES

CONTENTS

CATSUPS

PRESERVES

CONTENTS

JELLIES

CONFECTIONS

CHEESE

THE BLUE GRASS
COOK BOOK

Breads

BEATEN BISCUITS

Miss Lyle

1 pint of flour,
1 rounded tablespoon of lard,
1 good pinch of salt.

Mix with very cold sweet milk to a stiff dough.
Work 150 times through a kneader. Roll into
sheet one-half inch thick. Cut out or make out
with the hands. Stick with a fork and bake in a
hot oven about twenty minutes till a rich brown.

MT. AIRY BEATEN BISCUITS

Mrs. Simms

3 pints of flour sifted,
1 large kitchen spoon of lard,
1 teaspoon salt.

1

Have the lard *well chilled* on ice. Rub the lard into two pints of the flour. Make this into a stiff dough with ice water and a very little milk. Work through a kneader 150 times, gradually adding the other pint of flour, or till the dough is perfectly smooth. Roll out one-half inch thick, cut into biscuits, stick with a fork, and bake in a moderate oven till light brown. Serve hot.

BEATEN-BISCUIT SUG-GESTIONS

The dough can be kept for two days if put in a tightly covered jar and kept on ice or in a cool place. Roll from 150 to 200 times through the kneader. Bake from twenty to twenty-five minutes in a hot oven. If the stove is hot enough to blister them before they are baked, place a bread-pan on the upper grating. Many of the best housekeepers prefer the old way of making the biscuits out by hand to the use of the cutter.

BROWN BISCUITS

Mrs. John W. Fox

1 quart of new flour, unbolted or Graham flour,
2 tablespoons lard or butter,

2

1 cup of buttermilk with one teaspoon soda,
½ teaspoon salt,
2 teaspoons brown sugar.

Make this into soft dough, work little, roll out, and cut into biscuits and bake in a quick oven.

CREAM BISCUITS

Mrs. Henry C. Buckner

Mix 1 quart of flour,
5 ounces butter,
2 teaspoons of baking-powder and a little salt very
    lightly together,
Add one quart of sweet cream, and work very well
    for several minutes.

Roll out as thick as a silver dollar. Cook in hot oven. Serve hot with honey or preserves.

DIXIE BISCUITS

Mrs. Charles Ellet Cabell

3 pints of flour,
2 eggs,
1 small cup of yeast,
1 cup of sweet milk,
2 tablespoons lard,
1 teaspoon of salt.

3

Mix up the bread at eleven o'clock and let it rise. At four o'clock roll out and cut into biscuits two sizes, putting the small one on top and let it rise till supper. Bake twenty minutes.

FRENCH BISCUIT

Mrs. Joseph Holt

4 pints of flour,
4 eggs,
4 teaspoons of sugar,
1 tablespoonful of butter,
1 teacup of yeast,
1 pint of sweet milk.

Work it well and let it rise. Work it the second time and roll the dough thin. Cut out the biscuit, lard one side and place one on top of another and let it rise again.

SODA BISCUITS

1 quart flour,
1 pint of buttermilk,
1 tablespoon lard,
½ teaspoon soda,
½ teaspoon salt,

Make into biscuits and bake quickly.

4

BREAD-CRUMB BATTER CAKES FOR BREAKFAST

One pint of bread-crumbs, moistened with milk several hours before using. When ready to use, beat an egg separately and add

> 1 pinch of salt,
> 1 pint of buttermilk,
> 1 teaspoon of soda.

Mix well and add 1 large spoon of flour to make them turn well. Fry as you would any other batter cake.

If wanted particularly nice, take half buttermilk and half cream, instead of all buttermilk, or use sweet milk with baking-powder and omit soda.

BREAD FRITTERS

E. D. P.

1 quart of sweet milk,
2 teacups of bread-crumbs,
2 tablespoons of sugar,
1 small teaspoon of soda,
2 teaspoons of cream of tartar, dissolved in warm
water,
2 eggs,
nutmeg and salt to taste.

5

Boil the milk and soak the bread-crumbs. Add sugar, then yolks of eggs, etc., and put soda and cream of tartar last. Beat the 2 whites in last.

BROWN BREAD

V. C. G.

Set a sponge just as for white bread. Instead of adding white flour, make of equal parts of graham and rye flour. One cup of black molasses and water enough to moisten. Stir with a spoon, and do not knead as white bread. Bake in pans.

BUCKWHEAT CAKES

For breakfast cakes the batter must be made and put to rise the night before in a warm place.

1 quart buckwheat flour,
4 tablespoons yeast,
1 teaspoon salt,
1 tablespoon molasses,
Warm water enough to make a thin batter.

If the batter should be sour when ready for use, add a little soda. Serve with syrup or honey.

CORN BREAD
BATTER BREAD

Mrs. Cyrus McCormick

1 cup of boiled rice,
1 pint of sifted meal,
2 well-beaten eggs,
A little salt,
Small piece of melted butter or lard,
1 teaspoon baking-powder,
Sweet milk to make a rather thin batter.

Pour in a well-greased earthen baking dish and bake a half hour or more in a hot oven.

KENTUCKY BATTER BREAD

1 pint meal,
3 eggs,
1 teaspoon salt,
1 tablespoon melted butter.

Make a thin batter with sweet milk. Pour in a baking-dish and bake ¾ of an hour, or till it is a rich brown.

SOFT BATTER BREAD

Mrs. H. C. McDowell

1 quart sweet milk,
1 pint sour cream or buttermilk,
1 pint of corn meal,
1 teaspoon soda,
1 dessertspoon salt,
6 eggs,
1 lump of butter size of an egg.

Bring milk to the boiling point, add the meal gradually until it is like thin mush, add butter and salt and let it cool. Then add some cream in which soda is dissolved, then the eggs well beaten separately and bake in a moderate oven. Cover till it is risen. This amount is sufficient for 8 people.

MARCELLUS'S CORN MUFFINS (No. 1)

1 pint buttermilk,
½ pint corn meal,
1 teaspoon soda,
½ teaspoon salt,
1 egg,
1 tablespoon melted lard.

8

Beat the egg, add soda to buttermilk and 1 tablespoon melted lard and mix together. Have muffin-rings hot and well greased and fill half full and cook brown.

CORN MUFFINS (No. 2)

1 pint of buttermilk,
½ pint of white corn meal,
1 teaspoon of soda,
½ teaspoon of salt,
1 egg,
1 large kitchen spoon of rich cream,
1 large kitchen spoon of cooked rice or grits.

Mash the hominy till very smooth. Add salt, egg, and cream. Mix buttermilk and soda and pour in mixture. Beat the meal in last. Don't make the batter too stiff. Have muffin-rings hot and well greased. Fill nearly full and bake in a hot, quick oven.

MARCELLUS'S CORN-MEAL BATTER CAKES

1 tablespoon lard,
1 pint corn meal,
¾ pint of sour milk,

9

1 small teaspoon soda in milk and stir till it foams,

1 egg,

$\frac{1}{2}$ teaspoon salt.

Beat egg and pour milk over it and add meal. Then mix in the melted lard, 1 tablespoonful. Have griddle very hot and well greased and put on with spoon in small cakes and fry.

EGG BREAD

Pour a little boiling water over 1 quart of meal to scald it. Add a teaspoon of salt and stir in yolks of 3 eggs, 1 cup of milk, 1 tablespoon of lard, and butter melted. Add the well-beaten whites last.

Bake in moderate oven till well done—nearly an hour.

JOHNNIE CAKE

1 quart meal,

1 pint warm water,

1 teaspoon salt.

Sift meal in a pan and add water and salt. Stir it until it is light, and then place on a new, clean board and place nearly upright before the fire. When brown, cut in squares, butter nicely, and serve hot.

MAKING KENTUCKY CORN DODGERS

KENTUCKY CORN DODGERS

Favorite Dinner Bread

Mrs. Simms

Sift the best meal made from the white corn, any quantity desired. Salt to taste. Mix with cold water into stiff dough and form into round, long dodgers with the hands. Take the soft dough and form into shape by rolling between the hands, making the dodgers about 4 or 5 inches long and 1½ inches in diameter. Have a griddle hot, grease a little with lard, and put the dodgers on as you roll them. Put in oven and bake thoroughly, when they will be crisp and a rich brown.

This bread does not rise.

CORN DODGERS

1 pint of white corn meal, sifted,
½ teaspoon of salt,
enough fresh milk, with
2 tablespoons of cream, to mix it well into dodgers
    with the hands.

Have griddle very hot; sprinkle with a little meal, and as soon as it browns lay the bread on and cook in a hot oven till a crisp rich brown.

11

SPOON CORN BREAD

3 eggs,
nearly a quart of buttermilk,
1 teacup of sweet milk,
a light teaspoonful of soda,
lard the size of a walnut,
4 or 5 large spoonfuls of corn meal (after it is
    sifted).

Bake in an earthen dish an hour. Serve with a spoon.

HANOVER ROLLS

Miss Dabney

Sift twice 2 quarts of flour,
Add 4 tablespoons yeast,
Add 1 tablespoon lard or butter,
1 tablespoon sugar,
1 dessertspoon salt and a pinch of soda.

Use enough lukewarm water to make the mass soft enough to knead well, and put where it will rise. When light, grease the hands and make into rolls. Let it rise again and then bake.

HOW TO MAKE BREAD

Mrs. John C. Berryman

1 cup of yeast,
1 quart of flour,
1 teaspoon of lard,
1 teaspoon of salt,
1 teaspoon of granulated sugar,
$\frac{1}{2}$ pint of water.

Put the yeast, lard, salt, and sugar in the flour, then the water. Work till it blisters, which will take from 15 to 20 minutes. Put in a little lard on top and put in a wooden bowl. Let it rise from 5 to 6 hours, then make out into rolls. Let them rise for $1\frac{1}{2}$ hours, then bake in a quick oven.

If for loaves, they will require 2 hours for second rising and a moderate oven for baking.

LAPLANDS

1 pint milk,
$\frac{1}{2}$ pint flour,
2 eggs,
1 dessertspoon lard.

Beat separately and light as for cake. Bake in small shallow pans.

LIGHT ROLLS

2 pints flour,
1 tablespoon of sugar,
1 teaspoon salt,
2 eggs,
½ cup of lard,
½ cup of home-made yeast.

First mix lard, flour, and sugar. Then stir in other ingredients. Add enough milk and warm water to make thin batter. Set in warm place to rise, and then work in flour to make pretty stiff dough and very smooth. If put to rise at 12, will be ready at 6. Don't work much last time. Make out in pretty shape and put to rise, and bake in quick oven.

MUFFINS

Mrs. Richard H. Hanson

4 eggs,
1 quart sweet milk,
1 quart flour,
1 tablespoon melted butter,
A little salt.

Beat the eggs separately. Add milk and butter to yolks and then the flour. Add whites last and bake in hot muffin-irons.

14

CREAM MUFFINS

1½ pints flour,

2 eggs.

Use whites of eggs only. Mix eggs and little cream, little salt, and then the flour. Use enough cream to make batter right consistency. Grease muffin-irons. When hot, pour half full and bake quickly.

MARCELLUS'S WHEAT MUFFINS

2 cups flour,

2 teaspoons baking-powder,

1 teaspoon salt,

2 tablespoons melted butter,

2 tablespoons sugar,

1 cup milk,

1 well-beaten egg,

Bake in muffin tins and serve hot.

POPOVERS

Mrs. Ellet Cabell

Beat 2 eggs very stiff and add 1 cup of milk, 1 cup of flour, and a pinch of salt. Have small tins very hot and well buttered. Fill half full with the mixture, bake in a quick oven 20 minutes and eat at once.

RICE CAKES

Cook 1 cup of rice, and add to it $\frac{1}{2}$ cup of cream, 1 teaspoon baking-powder, 2 tablespoons flour, 2 eggs, well beaten. Fry in lard or butter just enough to grease skillet.

RUSK OR SWEET BREAD

1 pint of flour,
1 pint of white sugar,
1 teacup of melted lard,
$1\frac{1}{2}$ pints of water,
2 kitchen spoons of yeast.

Make into a batter at night, set in a warm place to rise. The next morning work into this sponge

2 beaten eggs,
3 pints of flour.

Set in a warm place to rise again. When light, make into pretty shapes; let rise again, and when light, bake. Spread on the rolls when warm white of an egg and sifted cinnamon.

The dough should be as soft as you can make it to work well.

SALLY LUNN (No. 1)

1 teaspoon salt,
1 quart flour,
1 pint of sweet milk,
½ cup of sugar,
1 small cup of yeast.

Make a batter and put in warm place to rise, and in 3 hours, when it is light enough, add 5 eggs which have been beaten separately, ½ cup of melted butter. Add ½ pint flour to make a stiff batter. Spread in pans 1 inch thick, and let rise, then bake. Serve two at a time with melted butter between.

SALLY LUNN (No. 2)

Bake Sally Lunn exactly as a loaf of bread, with steady heat. It requires a longer time, however. Do not make the batter too thin.

1 pint of milk,
3 eggs,
1 tablespoon of butter or nice sweet lard,
1 dessertspoon of sugar,
1 small teacup of yeast, and flour to make batter thick enough for the spoon to stand straight. This makes delicious drop muffins. If the batter is too thin it is apt to fall before it is thoroughly baked

and leave the inside of it a dough; if too thick, it
is only French rolls.

SALLY LUNN (No. 3)

Mrs. Cyrus McCormick

1½ pints flour,
3 eggs,
1 tablespoon white sugar,
½ cup melted butter,
1 teacup yeast,
1 pint milk.

Make into a stiff batter, having beaten ingredients well together. Let it rise for 5 hours. Then
add ½ teaspoon of soda in a little warm water and
pour the batter in a well-greased cake mould.
Bake 40 minutes and serve hot with butter.

SALT-RISING BREAD (No. 1)

⅔ pint of milk,
2 tablespoons of corn meal,
1 teaspoon of salt,
1 tablespoon of lard,
1 tablespoon of white sugar.

Pour boiling milk over salt and meal and stir
well. Set to rise at night. Next morning add

hot water to warm it; then flour enough to make it thick. Then add sugar and melted lard.

Mould in loaves and put to rise in a warm place. When risen, bake in moderately hot oven.

SALT-RISING BREAD (No. 2)

1 pint of new milk, which boil and thicken with meal. Keep in a warm place 12 hours. Pour in a teacup of lukewarm water, then stir in flour enough to make thick batter. Set the batter in kettle of warm water to rise and it will be high enough in 2 hours. Then take 6 pints of flour and 1 teacup of butter or lard, after having mixed batter with flour, and knead all thoroughly. Put in pans and let it rise, and then bake till it is light brown. Open door of oven and let the bread stand for a while till it is soaked well.

STEAM PONE

Mrs. John W. Fox

1 teacup New Orleans molasses,
5 teacups corn meal,
2 teacups brown flour,
1 teaspoon salt,

1 quart buttermilk,

2 teaspoons soda.

Mix thoroughly and place in air-tight bucket. Set in kettle of boiling water and boil for 6 hours. Then take from bucket, put in pan and bake slowly for 2 hours till a rich brown.

WAFFLES (No. 1)

Mrs. R. H. Hanson

1 quart flour, a little salt,

1 quart buttermilk,

1 pint melted lard,

1 heaping teaspoon soda,

1 egg.

As the success of the waffles depends on the mixing, the directions must be followed carefully.

First, put the flour and salt in a pan and beat the buttermilk into it. Add the egg, which has been well beaten. Then add the hot lard. Beat the mixture thoroughly, and lastly add the dry soda. Add nothing after the soda is in. Beat all well and bake in *hot* waffle-irons that have been *well greased.*

Use half this quantity for an ordinary sized family.

WAFFLES (No. 2)

Miss Dabney

1 pint sour cream,
1 pint flour,
3 eggs,
½ teaspoon soda.

Beat well and fill hot waffle-irons, which have been well buttered. Cook till a rich crisp brown and serve hot with melted butter. Be sure to have *irons hot.*

YEAST

½ gallon of water,
4 large potatoes,
½ cup of salt,
½ cup of sugar,
1 tablespoon of hops,
1 cup of yeast.

Put the sugar and salt in the water and put hops in a little muslin bag and drop in the water. Let it boil, then grate potatoes and stir in. Let it simmer till it thickens. Remove from stove, and when it is milk cold add 1 cup of good yeast. Let it remain near the fire to rise. Keep in glass jar in a cool place. Use ½ cup of yeast to 1 quart of flour.

Eggs

BAKED EGGS

Hard boil the eggs and cut into slices. Put a layer of eggs in a baking-dish well buttered, then add bread-crumbs with pieces of butter throughout. Season with salt and pepper and cover the top with crumbs and grated cheese and bake a rich brown.

BOILED EGGS

Boil 3 minutes for soft-boiled eggs,
Boil 5 minutes for hard-boiled eggs,
Boil 15 minutes for salad.

BREAKFAST EGGS

6 eggs,
3 tablespoons cream,
1 tablespoon butter,
Salt and pepper to taste.

23

Put butter in a hot baking-dish. After breaking the eggs one at a time in a saucer, slip carefully into the hot baking-dish. Add the cream and sprinkle salt and pepper over them. Cook 5 minutes and serve hot in the baking-dish.

EGGS À LA CRÊME

Boil eggs hard, cut in slices and lay on a dish, add a layer of grated bread-crumbs, a little salt and pepper, and a pint of milk or cream. Let it boil. While boiling, stir in a tablespoon of butter with a tablespoon of flour mashed in it. Let it mix well; then pour over the eggs, and bake a few minutes.

EGGS WITH TOMATO SAUCE

Take ½ dozen small ripe tomatoes, remove the skins and stew them. Strain and season with salt, pepper, 1 tablespoon butter, and add a pinch of soda. Return to the fire and add 2 tablespoons flour and boil till thick. Scramble the eggs and pour the sauce around them and serve at once.

OMELET

6 eggs beaten separately,
1 cup of milk,
1 tablespoon of butter.

Mix milk, yolks, butter, salt, and pepper, and add the whites last. Pour into a hot pan which has been well buttered, and cook quickly on top of oven. When it begins to thicken, put inside the oven and brown. Cut in half and roll and serve hot at once. All omelets should be served immediately.

MARCELLUS'S OMELET

4 eggs beaten separately,
1 cup of bread-crumbs,
1 teaspoon butter, salt and pepper to taste,
1 cup of milk.

Add the milk to the yolks, also the crumbs and other ingredients. Beat the whites in last. Have the skillet moderately hot, pour in and cook till it settles. Then bake in oven till a rich brown. Double the omelet and serve at once.

OMELET, SPANISH STYLE

Fry a little garlic in sweet oil, in a tin or porcelain pan, having previously chopped it very fine; when the garlic is done, add some sliced tomatoes, sliced mushrooms, and smoked beef tongue; season well. Make a plain omelet; fry it in sweet oil and put the garlic, tomatoes, mushrooms, and tongue inside; cool and serve with a little tomato sauce.

VERY FINE OMELET

4 eggs,
1 cup of milk,
1 tablespoon butter,
1½ tablespoons of grated ham,
1 tablespoon of chopped parsley,
1 tablespoon of flour.

Boil the milk and make a paste of the flour by adding a little milk and put into the boiling milk. Add salt, pepper, and butter, and set aside to cool. Beat the eggs separately and add the yolks, parsley, and ham to the milk. Add the whites last. Bake till a rich brown and serve at once.

POACHED EGGS (No. 1)

Mrs. H. C. McDowell

Add a little salt to the white of an egg and beat dry. Turn into a buttered glass and put the yolk on a nest in the middle of it. Put the glass on trivet in lukewarm water. Cover and let stand till the egg is set and rises in the glass. Do not let water around glass boil. Serve at once.

POACHED EGGS (No. 2)

Have water boiling hot and add a little salt. Break the eggs carefully into the water, one at a time, and let them cook 3 minutes. Serve on thin, crisp toast.

SCALLOPED EGGS

1 egg for each person,
Salt and pepper,
For 1 dozen eggs, 1 cup of bread-crumbs,
1 pint milk.

Boil the eggs hard and slice and place in a buttered dish, first a layer of eggs and then a layer of crumbs, with pieces of butter throughout and salt and pepper to taste. Cover the top with crumbs, pour over the pint of milk, and bake till brown.

SCRAMBLED EGGS

Have the skillet hot and add 1 tablespoon butter. Break the eggs and drop in, stirring constantly, pepper and salt and cook quickly. Serve immediately on toast or with crisp bacon.

SHIRRED EGGS

Take 6 fresh eggs. Grease baking-dish with butter. Do not beat the eggs, but break and pour them in the dish. Salt and pepper them and put in a hot oven and cook till the whites curl up. Serve in baking-dish at once.

STUFFED EGGS

1 dozen eggs.

Boil and peel and cut into halves. Remove the yolks and cream them and add 1 tablespoon butter, 2 tablespoons old ham, nicely minced. Season highly with salt, pepper, and mustard, and a little chopped onion. Fill the eggs and arrange on a dish or a platter.

Soups

ASPARAGUS SOUP

3 bunches of asparagus,
1 quart of cream or rich milk,
1 tablespoon of butter,
½ tablespoon flour.

Boil the asparagus in 1 quart salt water till tender. Drain water off, then add cream. Rub butter and flour together and add before taking from the stove. Add salt and pepper to taste. Serve with toasted bread or crackers.

BLACK BEAN SOUP

E. D. P.

1 ten-cent beef bone,
1 gallon of water,
Small bunch of parsley,
4 cloves,

Small bunch of celery tops,
1 carrot,
1 quart of black navy beans
Small teacup of sherry,

Boil the bone, cloves, celery, and parsley 4 hours the day before using, and next day skim all grease and run through sieve.

Add to this the beans, and boil till the beans are soft, and then mash through colander. Thicken with a little brown flour. To $\frac{1}{2}$ gallon put the small cup of sherry, and when serving put in each plate a thin slice of lemon and one slice of hard-boiled egg. Salt and pepper to taste.

CALF'S HEAD SOUP

Remove the brains from the calf's head. Put the head in 4 quarts of cold water and cook till meat drops from the bone—3 or 4 hours. Remove the bone and add:

3 onions, chopped fine,
6 cloves,
Salt and pepper to taste,
Boil an hour.

Season the brains with salt and pepper and butter and beat together with 1 raw egg. Make into balls, roll in egg and cracker dust, and fry a rich brown. Drop in tureen with 2 lemons sliced thin. Add 1 cup of catsup or wine to the soup and pour in tureen and serve at once.

CHESTNUT SOUP

E. D. P.

2 quarts of Spanish chestnuts,
2 quarts of chicken stock,
1 pint of rich cream,
Salt, nutmeg, and cayenne pepper to taste.

Shell the chestnuts, put them in a pan and cover with cold water. Let them scald until the inner skin can be taken off. Put them on a sieve to allow the hot water to drain off, and while draining, pour on some cold water, so as the skins can be removed with the hand. When they are well skinned put them into a saucepan with the chicken stock, and let them simmer until perfectly tender. Then mash through the sieve into the same stock. Season with nutmeg, salt, and cayenne pepper to the taste. Put it into a saucepan with hot water underneath, stirring all the time until it begins to simmer; then pour in the pint of cream, and after stirring 5 minutes longer, serve.

CLAM SOUP

24 clams,
½ gallon water,
2 tablespoons butter,
2 onions,
Salt and pepper to taste.

Chop the clams and use the meat and liquor and add the water. Do not boil, but cook gently till it begins to thicken. Season, and just before taking from the stove add 1 pint cream or rich milk. Pour in tureen, add a little parsley, and serve at once.

CLEAR SOUP OR BOUILLON

E. D. P.

Cut up the lean of coarse beef into small pieces.
1 good-sized onion,
1 good-sized carrot,   Peel and cut up before
1 good-sized turnip.   using.
Salt, nutmeg, and cayenne pepper to taste,
4 whole cloves.

Fry with 1 tablespoon of butter in soup-kettle. When it begins to look whitish, pour over it the stock from 1 chicken. Boil the chicken in 1 gallon of water in early morning, and make stock in afternoon. Boil 1 hour, strain and put away till next day for aspic or bouillon.

For bouillon, beat an egg and let it come to a boil in the bouillon, and strain before serving.

CORN SOUP (No. 1)

1 can of corn,
1 quart of boiling milk,
Butter, salt, and pepper to taste.

Press the corn through the colander and add to the quart of boiling milk, and season to taste. Serve hot with toast in squares.

MRS. DAVENPORT'S CORN SOUP (No. 2)

12 ears of corn,
1½ pints of water,
2 pints new milk,
2 eggs,
2 tablespoons of butter,
1 tablespoon of flour.

Split and cut off the corn, which you must boil in the water until done and the water is nearly exhausted; then add the milk and let it come to a

boil, some of which pour in the beaten eggs and
return to the kettle; work flour with the butter,
with pepper and salt to taste; stir into the soup
and then serve.

CREAM OF CELERY SOUP

E. D. P.

1 quart of chicken soup,
1 dessertspoonful of butter,
1 dessertspoonful of cornstarch,
3 heads of celery,
1 quart of milk or cream.

Take the white part of the celery and chop it as
fine as possible. Put it to boil with the milk, and
let it cook until it can be rubbed through a sieve.
If too thick, after it has been rubbed through, add
a little more milk. Return it to the pot, and add
the chicken soup. When it has boiled about 10
minutes, rub the butter and cornstarch together,
and stir in until it thickens; then season to the taste
with salt and white pepper.

GUMBO SOUP

1 chicken,
2 pints okra,

1 pint tomatoes,
1 tablespoon butter.

Fry the chicken and pour over ½ gallon of boiling water and cook till the meat drops from the bones. Remove bones. Prepare the vegetables and add to the soup and boil. Then add thickening and season to taste, or as for any other soup. Before pouring off add the butter. Add hot water as it boils down. Serve hot, with rice boiled dry.

CHICKEN GUMBO

Mrs. Simms

Fry 1 chicken. When done, cover with boiling water and cook until it is ready to fall apart. Remove the chicken, place in a dish to cool, and pour the liquor into the soup-pot. Add chicken, minced or shredded very fine.

Fry 1 onion with 1 slice of fat pork. Rinse the skillet out with a little water and pour all into the soup. Put 1 can of tomatoes on to boil with 2 quarts of water. Slice ½ green pepper and 1 small red pepper very fine and add to tomatoes. Boil 2 hours. Take 2 cans of okra, carefully removing all the tough pods, ½ cup of rice, and 1 tablespoon of minced parsley. Add to the soup and boil 1 hour longer. Season with salt and black pepper to taste.

In summer 2 or 3 ears of corn, cut and scraped, make a nice addition. If desired, serve with 1 spoonful of boiled rice to each soup plate.

OYSTER GUMBO

E. D. P.

1 large chicken,
1 can of oysters,
½ pound of boiled ham,
2 quarts of boiling water,
1 bunch of summer savory,
1 bunch of parsley,
1 tablespoonful of filée powder,
Salt, black and cayenne pepper to the taste.

Divide the chicken, skin and flour each piece well; cut the ham in dice, and, with a cooking-spoonful of butter, fry until brown. Then pour on it 2 quarts of boiling water, the bunches of summer savory and parsley tied together, salt and cayenne pepper. Let this boil slowly for 4 hours. Take out the summer savory and parsley, pull the chicken to pieces, return it to the pot, and about 15 minutes before serving heat the oysters and

"BROAD, PORTLY, KIND OF HEART"

their liquor, and add to the soup. While they are simmering very slowly take out a teacupful of the soup and mix with the filée powder. When perfectly smooth put it in the soup; let it boil up once and it will be done. Pour into a heated tureen and serve with some nicely boiled rice in another dish.

JULIENNE SOUP

V. C. G.

2 quarts clear stock,
½ pint carrots cut small,
¼ pint onions,
½ pint turnips,
½ head of celery.

Bleach the vegetables a few minutes in boiling water, then let them simmer in the soup until tender. Season with salt and pepper.

KENTUCKY BURGOUT

Mrs. Garrard

6 squirrels,
6 birds,
1½ gallons of water,
1 teacup of pearl barley,
1 quart of tomatoes,

37

1 quart of corn,
1 quart of oysters,
1 pint of sweet cream,
¼ pound of butter,
2 tablespoons of flour,
Season to taste.

Boil the squirrels and birds in the water till tender and remove all the bones. Add barley and vegetables and cook slowly for 1 hour. Ten minutes before serving add the oysters and cream with butter and flour rubbed together. Season and serve hot.

OKRA SOUP

Take ½ gallon of beef stock, 1 quart of tomatoes, and 1 quart of okra, and pepper and salt to taste and boil ½ hour. Thicken with 1 tablespoon of flour.

OYSTER SOUP (No. 1)
(*Famous Virginia Recipe*)

Miss Virginia Croxton

3 pints oysters,
1½ pints milk,
2 eggs,
Piece of butter size of an egg,

1   slice of lean ham,
1   stalk of celery or pinch of celery seed.

Pour oysters in colander and put the strained liquor in a kettle and add enough water for quantity desired.   Add salt, pepper, celery, and ham. When it boils up, skim off the foamy substance. Drop the oysters in and let boil a few minutes, then the beaten eggs and milk and little thickening of flour made with part of the milk.   Add the butter last and let all boil up once, stirring to prevent eggs from curdling.   Pour in tureen over small squares of toast and serve immediately.

OYSTER SOUP (No. 2)

Take 1 quart of rich milk or cream and boil. Draw off 1 quart of oysters and boil and skim. Add it and the oysters to boiling milk and cook 5 minutes.   Powder 1 dozen crackers, and with them put $\frac{1}{2}$ cup of butter in soup tureen and pour over and serve hot.   Pepper and salt to taste.

OX-TAIL SOUP

Cut 1 tail into pieces and add:
1 gallon water,
1 teaspoon of salt,
As it boils, remove the scum.

39

When meat is done, remove the tail and add:

1 bunch of celery cut fine,

2 small onions,

4 carrots,

4 cloves,

Pepper to taste,

Cook till the vegetables are tender.

Remove meat from the tail and place in tureen, pour soup over it and serve very hot.

PEA SOUP (No. 1)

Two pints of shelled peas, $\frac{1}{2}$ chicken; put on with $1\frac{1}{2}$ gallons of water, some thyme, parsley, salt and pepper. When the peas are done, take them out, then return them to the water in the mashed state. Add $\frac{1}{4}$ pound of butter rolled in flour.

Before sending to table add $\frac{1}{2}$ pint of cream.

PEA SOUP (No. 2)

1 can peas,

1 quart boiling milk,

1 tablespoon butter.

Press the peas through a colander and add to a quart of boiling milk. Add to this 1 tablespoon butter, and salt and pepper to taste.

MARCELLUS'S POTATO SOUP
(No. 1)

3 large-sized potatoes,
Butter,
1 cup of cream,
Salt and pepper to taste.

Cut the potatoes up in fine pieces and boil 2 hours in 2 quarts of water. Add seasoning and piece of butter size of an egg and 1 cup of cream. Serve hot.

POTATO SOUP (No. 2)

1 quart of potatoes,
2 ounces of butter,
2 pints milk,
4 eggs.

Boil the potatoes soft, and smooth with a little boiling water until a thin batter. Stir the butter, pepper, and salt to taste into the milk. Beat the eggs and add to potatoes. When milk boils, pour over the potatoes and do not return to the fire.

PURÉE OF CHICKEN

E. D. P.

1 large chicken,
1 small knuckle of veal,
3 quarts of water,
¼ pound of rice,
1 bunch of parsley,
1 blade of mace,
½ teaspoonful of celery seed,
1 coffeecupful of boiling cream,
Salt and pepper to the taste.

Put the chicken and veal on with 3 quarts of water, together with the rice, parsley, mace, and the celery seed, tied in a muslin bag. Boil gently until the chicken is thoroughly done, taking care to skim well all the time it is boiling. Take out the veal, bone, cut, and pound the chicken in a mortar; moisten it with a little of the stock, and pass it through the colander. Strain the stock, pressing the rice through the sieve. Return the chicken to the stock, season, and just before serving, pour in the cream. Heat thoroughly, but don't boil.

SALSIFY SOUP

1 quart of salsify cooked in water till tender,
1 quart of new milk. Mash the salsify through
sieve.

Add to boiling milk 1 tablespoon flour and 1
large tablespoon butter. Pour all together and
season with pepper and salt.

SIMPLE CHICKEN SOUP

E. D. P.

1 coffeecupful of cream,
1 teacupful of well-boiled rice,
1 blade of mace,
1 saltspoonful of celery seed,
1 dessertspoonful of cornstarch.

When boiling a pair of chickens for dinner, put
in the water a blade of mace and a saltspoonful of
celery seed. After the chickens are done, take out
2 quarts of the water; skim well, and add the
cream or rich milk; then the rice and the dessertspoonful of cornstarch; season to the taste. It
will require about 3 quarts of water for a pair of
chickens.

43

SOUP STOCK OF BEEF

E. D. P.

1 large shin-bone,
4 quarts of water,
2 pounds of lean beef,
4 carrots,
3 onions,
4 turnips,
1 bunch of parsley,
1 teaspoonful of celery seed,
Salt to the taste.

Put the bone, which has been previously cracked in 3 pieces, into the soup-pot, with the water, and beef cut into pieces the size of an egg, and some salt. Boil slowly for 1 hour, skimming well until all of the grease is taken off. Scrape the carrots, peel the onions and turnips, then quarter, and, with the celery seed, add to the soup. Let this boil slowly for 4 hours; take off, strain into a stone jar, and keep in a cool place. Veal stock can be made in the same way, by getting a large knuckle of veal and adding 2 pounds of the meat.

TOMATO SOUP

1 quart of peeled fresh tomatoes or canned. Let them stew till thoroughly cooked and add half a teaspoon of soda. Have ½ gallon of fresh milk boiling. Stir into the tomatoes 1 tablespoon of butter, 1 of flour, and red pepper and salt to taste. Pour tomatoes into milk and let it boil 15 minutes. Serve hot.

TURTLE SOUP

1 turtle weighing 4 or 5 pounds,
1 gallon cold water,
1 onion,
4 cloves,
2 tablespoons butter,
Salt and pepper to taste,
½ tablespoon flour,
1 glass of claret or Madeira wine,
2 lemons.

Boil the turtle in the water till the meat drops from the bones; 3 or 4 hours will be required. Add the seasoning and boil 30 minutes. Roll butter and flour together and add just before taking from the fire. Pour in tureen and add wine and lemons thinly sliced. Serve at once.

MOCK-TURTLE SOUP (No. 1)

4 pounds lean beef,
½ gallon cold water.

Boil till tender and remove the meat and chop fine. Put back in liquor and add:

2 onions,
6 cloves,
Salt and pepper to taste,
1 tablespoon celery seed,
1 tablespoon butter and ½ flour.

Thicken with flour and butter rubbed together. Pour in tureen and add 1 cup of good catsup and serve at once.

MOCK-TURTLE SOUP (No. 2)

Miss Elise White

1 calf's head,
2 bunches of celery,
Yolks of 6 eggs,
1 lemon,
1 cup walnut catsup,
1 teaspoon cloves,
1 onion chopped fine,
Salt and pepper to taste.

46

Boil the head in plenty of water till tender. Strain and add to the liquor the ingredients, and flavor with sherry or wine. Boil eggs hard and slice and add to soup.

VEGETABLE SOUP (No. 1)

Take a 10-cent soup-bone and put it in $1\frac{1}{2}$ gallons water and let boil slowly for 5 hours. When cool, add 4 potatoes cut in small pieces, 4 tomatoes, 4 ears of corn, and 2 onions. Season with salt and pepper to taste, and let it cook slowly for 3 hours. Then thicken with 2 tablespoons flour. Serve hot.

VEGETABLE SOUP (No. 2)

Have good strong stock which has been made the day before. Strain in the kettle and add:

1 carrot,
1 small cabbage,
1 tablespoon rice,
1 onion,
3 tomatoes.

Chop all ingredients very fine. Boil 1 hour. Serve with small toasted squares. For clear soup, strain and leave all the ingredients out.

Fish

BAKED FISH (No. 1)

V. C. G.

Rub inside of fish with salt. Add pepper and salt on outside with slices of onion and pickled pork. Then dredge with flour and put in the pan with 1 quart of boiling water. Bake well and baste often. When cooked, place the pan on top of stove.

If gravy is not thick enough, add a piece of floured butter the size of an egg or smaller. Stir in a half-bottle of tomato catsup and pour over fish. Remove onion and pork before serving.

BAKED FISH (No. 2)

Mrs. Tom R. Wyles

1 small fish,
1 cup of bread-crumbs,
Moisten with hot water,

1 teaspoon melted butter,
1 teaspoon Worcestershire sauce,
1 teaspoon tomato catsup,
1 teaspoon minced parsley,
1 teaspoon minced onion,
1 teaspoon minced pickle or olives,
1 teaspoon lemon juice.
Salt, pepper, and paprika to taste.

Make the mixture very moist, and add water if necessary. Stuff the fish and tie securely and bake.

FISH À LA CRÊME

V. C. G.

Dress cold, boiled fish with this sauce:

Take 2 tablespoons of flour, and add by degrees 1 quart of milk, 2 tablespoons of finely minced onion, the same of parsley, plenty of salt and pepper, enough to make it sharp. Stir this over the fire until it begins to thicken, then stir in $\frac{1}{2}$ teacup of butter.

Put some of the sauce at the bottom of the baking-dish, then a layer of fish, and so on till it is all used, finishing with sauce and a light layer of bread-crumbs, and bake till a little brown.

FISH IN SHELLS

Take a nice white fish and let it boil ½ hour; then pick it very fine, removing skin and bones. Make a dressing of 1 large cup of rich cream, 1 tablespoon of butter, a little flour, and put in saucepan and stir till thick. Add seasoning, salt and pepper and a little celery, and mix with the fish.

Fill the shells. Sprinkle bread-crumbs and tiny pieces of butter on top, and put in oven and brown.

LOBSTER À LA DABNEY

V. C. G.

Pick the meat from 2 good-sized lobsters, leaving with it some of the soft part. Put 1 quart of milk over boiling water, removing 1 gill to mix with 1 gill of flour. When the milk is scalding hot, stir this in. Season with red pepper and salt to taste.

Stir until the flour is cooked; then pour it on the lobster and mix well. It must be softer than for salad. Put in shallow pans or shells; cover with bread-crumbs; dot with butter and bake till brown.

This can be prepared in the morning for tea.

SALMON

1 pint can of salmon,
½ cup of crackers rolled coarse,
2 tablespoons butter,
3 well-beaten eggs,
Salt and pepper.

Steam one hour; serve with drawn butter poured over it, in which put chopped mushrooms a few minutes before taking from the stove. Chopped olives and capers are an improvement.

BAKED SHAD

Miss Virginia Croxton

Clean, open, and take out the roe, if there is one. Wash carefully and scrape out the blood near the backbone. Lay in a pan long enough not to bend the fish with head on. Fill with seasoned bread-crumbs and sprinkle well in and out with pepper and salt. Gash the top about 2 inches apart and lay strips of fat bacon in the gashes. Bake in a hot oven, adding hot water enough to keep fish from drying and sticking to the pan. Bake from ½ to an hour, according to size. Serve with tomato catsup or Worcestershire sauce.

FRIED SHAD

Miss Virginia Croxton

Clean, split, and take out the backbone. Cut into pieces about 2 inches wide. Salt and pepper to taste and fry in hot lard until a light brown.

ROASTED SHAD

A Virginia Recipe

Wipe dry and rub inside and out with pepper and salt. Fasten the fish securely to a board and put in front of an open fire and let it cook till well done. Serve with drawn butter.

TURBOT

Steam 1 fish; pick to pieces and bone; sprinkle with salt and pepper in layers and set aside. Boil a little parsley and onion in a pint of milk; strain, set back on fire; stir in $\frac{1}{4}$ of a pound of flour, $\frac{1}{4}$ of a pound of butter, and boil till thick; set to one side until partially cold; beat up 2 eggs and stir in the mixture; butter a baking-dish and fill with alternate layers of fish and dressing; sprinkle top with bread-crumbs, and bake until it puffs up in centre.

Oysters

BROILED OYSTERS

Miss Virginia Croxton

Drain the oysters and free them from pieces of shells. Lay on cloth to dry. Season with salt and pepper. Broil on a greased griddle over a clear fire, or in a frying-pan with a little butter and lard mixed. When cooked to a light brown, turn and cook other side. Serve on hot toast.

CREAMED OYSTERS (No. 1)

E. D. P.

Boil 1 quart of cream and thicken with ½ dozen crackers. Season with 1 dessertspoon of butter, salt and pepper to taste.

When boiling pour in 1 quart of select oysters, and when the ends curl, remove from stove and serve hot with crackers.

CREAMED OYSTERS (No. 2)

Mrs. Charles Berryman

1 tablespoon of butter in chafing-dish,
1 can of oysters or 1 dozen fresh oysters.

Drop in the hot butter and let cook till edges curl.   Season with

Salt and pepper,
Juice of 1 lemon,
Yolks of 2 eggs beaten up with
2 tablespoons of cream.

Let cook till thick and serve on toast.

FRENCH STEWED OYSTERS

Fifty large oysters set over the fire in their liquor; skim well when they begin to simmer; take them out with a perforated ladle and throw them into cold water to plump them; when cold, place in wine, then drain them; add to the liquor ½ pound of butter divided into 4 pieces, well rolled in flour, ½ dozen blades of mace, ½ nutmeg grated, a salt-spoon of cayenne pepper; stir until the butter is melted and mixed, then put in the oysters; when they boil, take them off and stir in yolks of 3 eggs well beaten; serve hot.

FRIED OYSTERS (No. 1)

Miss Virginia Croxton

Drain large, plump oysters and free them from small pieces of shells. Lay them on a cloth to dry. Season with milk, salt, and pepper, and dip in beaten egg and roll in cracker dust. Fry a light brown in hot lard and serve at once.

FRIED OYSTERS (No. 2)

Choose large oysters and drain thoroughly in a colander. Dry in a towel. Dip each oyster first in sifted cracker-crumbs; then in egg (1 egg beaten with a large spoonful of cold water, $\frac{1}{2}$ a teaspoon of salt, a saltspoon of pepper, being enough for 2 dozen oysters). Roll again in crumbs, and lay them in a wire frying basket, and, holding the basket by the handle, dip into a kettle of boiling lard; use a porcelain kettle almost one-third full of lard. Dip the basket in and let it remain until the oysters are a light brown; then turn out on a piece of brown paper until they are so free from grease that they can be served in a napkin laid in the platter. The albumen in the egg makes a coating over the oyster so that the grease

57

cannot get to it. The lard can be set aside and used several times.

OYSTER COCKTAILS

Mrs. Mary Webb

2 dozen small oysters,
1 tablespoon horseradish,
½ teaspoon tabasco sauce,
1 tablespoon of vinegar,
1 tablespoon of Worcestershire sauce,
1 tablespoon tomato catsup,
½ teaspoon of salt.

Mix the sauce well and place on ice an hour before serving. Have oysters ice cold.

Put 3 or 4 oysters in a punch glass, and add 1 or 2 tablespoons of sauce to each glass.

OYSTER FRITTERS

Miss Virginia Croxton

1 pint small oysters or large ones chopped.

Make a stiff batter with 2 eggs, 1 teaspoon of yeast powder, and a little milk. Add oysters and flour to thicken. Salt to taste. Drop in spoonfuls in hot fat and fry a light brown.

OYSTER LOAF

A Creole Recipe

1 loaf of bread,
1 quart of oysters fried,
½ teacup of tomato catsup,
½ dozen small pickles or 1 dozen olives.

Cut off one end of loaf and remove the soft inside, leaving a shell, which thoroughly butter and place in oven to toast. Fill with a layer of hot fried oysters, a little catsup, and pickles or olives, another layer of oysters, till shell is filled. Fasten the top on, cut in slices, and serve very hot.

A nice supper dish after theatre.

OYSTER PATTIES

Put 1 pint of milk or cream on to boil and season with butter, mace, salt, and pepper, and thicken with spoon of cornstarch. When thick add 1 quart of fine oysters. Cook till edges curl. Make patties of rich puff paste, and when pastry is brown put 4 oysters in each shell with some of the sauce.

PICKLED OYSTERS

V. C. G.

Boil the oysters till the edges curl and the soft part is plump. Take off and let them cool in the juice. Remove the oysters and strain the juice, adding to it vinegar to the taste, whole black pepper, allspice, small piece of mace, and boil about 5 minutes.

Remove from stove, and when perfectly cold pour on the oysters.

Add wine to the taste, small red peppers, and salt.

SCALLOPED OYSTERS

Miss Virginia Croxton

1 quart oysters.

Cover the bottom of baking-dish with cracker-crumbs and put in a layer of oysters. Sprinkle with salt and pepper and bits of butter. Cover with cracker-crumbs and oysters till dish is full. Let the cracker-dust lie on top in a thick layer. Pour over this the oyster liquor, 1 cup milk, 1 beaten egg, and cook till oysters are well done.

VEAL AND OYSTERS

V. C. G.

Two pounds of tender, lean veal cut in thin, small pieces. Dredge with flour and fry in sufficient *hot* lard to keep it from sticking.

When nearly done add a pint and a half of fine oysters. Thicken with a little flour and season with salt and pepper, and cook till done.

Serve in a hot dish.

Entrees

ASPIC JELLY

4 pints of clear soup,
1 box of Cox's gelatine,
1 teacup of wine,
2 tablespoons of vinegar,
Salt and pepper to taste,
Whites of 2 eggs beaten to a stiff froth.

Stir all well while cooking till it begins to boil. See that the gelatine is well dissolved, so that it will not stick to bottom of kettle. Do not stir after it boils hard. When the eggs break away and the jelly looks clear, remove from stove and strain through a clean cloth. Have the cloth soaking in boiling water, and squeeze well out of the hot water before running the jelly through.

Put chicken in mould, pour sauce over while warm, and serve with truffles.

BOUDINS À LA RICHELIEU

E. D. P.

1 pound of raw turkey or chicken breast,
⅛ pound of panada,
½ pound of butter,
¼ pound of pickled pork,
3 eggs,
4 truffles,
Salt and pepper to taste.

Grind the turkey or chicken. Cream the butter with the panada and add the meat, having pork ground with the meat. Break in the eggs, one at a time, beating the mixture well. Slice a part of the truffles in this mixture, reserving the rest for the sauce. Pour in the liquor from the truffles. Put this in the Boudin moulld, place in bread-pan with water around, and boil ¾ of an hour.

Serve with champignon sauce.

CHICKEN ASPIC WITH WALNUTS

Mrs. Henry C. Buckner

Make a clear consomme; to 1½ cups of consomme add ½ box of Cox's gelatine soaked in ½

AUNT FRANCES, COOK AT AUVERGNE, PARIS, KY.

cup of water one-half hour; put one layer of jelly
¼ inch thick into a double mould and let chill; then
fill the outside mould with jelly; fill the centre
with 1½ cupfuls of celery cut rather fine and ½
a cup of English walnuts cut size of celery; mix
them with a dressing made of 3 tablespoons of
melted chicken jelly, 2 tablespoons of oil, 1 teaspoon of salt, 1 teaspoon vinegar, ½ teaspoon tarragon vinegar, ¼ teaspoon red pepper. Cover with
jelly so as to enclose the celery mixture; turn when
moulded on flat dish with shredded lettuce.

CHICKEN CUTLETS

Mrs. Henry C. Buckner

For a dozen and a half cutlets use a generous pint
of cooked chicken, chopped rather coarse, a cupful
of cream, 3 tablespoons of butter, 1 of flour, 1 teaspoon of salt, 4 level tablespoons of fine chopped
mushrooms, 4 eggs, 1 pint of sifted crumbs, ½ teaspoon of pepper, ½ teaspoon of onion juice, 1 teaspoonful of chopped parsley. Mix chicken with
the salt, pepper, onion juice, lemon juice, and
chopped mushrooms; put the cream on the stove in
a large frying-pan; beat the flour and butter to-

gether until smooth and light, and when the cream begins to boil, stir this into it; stir constantly until the sauce boils again; then add the seasoned chicken and cook for three minutes; beat two of the eggs until light and stir them into the boiling ingredients; take from the fire immediately and pour into a flat dish, to get very cold, for an hour or so. The colder the mixture becomes, the more easily the cutlets can be formed. Butter a cutlet mould thoroughly and sprinkle some crumbs into it; pack with the chicken, and then give the mould a tap on the table to make the cutlet drop out. The mould is buttered only once, but is sprinkled with crumbs each time a new cutlet is formed. When all the chicken has been used, beat the two remaining eggs in a deep plate and put some of the crumbs in another plate; drop the cutlets into the eggs first, and into the crumbs afterward; at serving time put them into a frying-basket, being careful not to crowd them, and cook in boiling fat for two minutes. Drain well and serve with white mushroom or Bechamel sauce. Mould with the hands if preferred.

COQUILLES OF CHICKEN

Mrs. Henry C. Buckner

> 1 chicken,
> 1 can of mushrooms,
> 1 tablespoon of flour.

Chop cold, boiled, or roasted chicken fine.

The mushrooms must be cut up, not chopped. Put liquor on for the mushrooms. Let it come to a boil, then add ½ as much cream as there is liquor. Stir well. Put pepper, salt, and tablespoonful of flour, and boil well. After shells are filled two-thirds full of the mixed chicken and mushrooms, pour dressing over it, cover top with cracker-dust and put in oven and brown.

CRÊME DE VOLAILLE (No. 1)

Mrs. B. F. Buckner

1 chicken, chopped very fine,
2 eggs,
½ teacup of cream,
½ teaspoon of thyme,
1 dessertspoon of the fat part of fresh pork, scraped with a knife,

Salt and pepper,
½ teaspoon of minced onion,
1 dessertspoon of parsley, chopped very fine.

Mix these ingredients together. To mould nicely it must be very stiff. Grease the mould, thoroughly lining it with the cream, leaving a space in the centre, and after putting in the mushrooms and white sauce—for which a recipe is given —steam 1½ hours.

Dissolve a tablespoon of gelatine in a very little hot water, and put a teaspoonful of it in the crême and the rest in the white sauce.

Of course it must be put in before it is put in the mould.

The following is to put in the space inside the crême in the centre of the mould:

1 tablespoon of butter,
1 tablespoon of flour,
½ pint of milk,
The remainder of the dissolved gelatine.

Stir while cooking, and add ½ of a can of chopped mushrooms.

Serve with white sauce for Crême de Volaille.

CRÊME DE VOLAILLE (No. 2)

Mrs. H. C. McDowell

1 pound raw chicken, without bones, skin, etc.,
½ teaspoon onion juice,
2 teaspoons parsley.

Run through the grinder till very fine. Cream into this ¼ pound butter, with salt and pepper to taste. Break in 3 raw eggs, 1 at a time, then beat it well as you would a delicate cake.

Line a mould with this, leaving a hole for the following:

Stew half a can of champignons in their own liquor, thicken with butter and flour. Cover the hole with some of the meat and steam 5 hours. The other half of the champignons stew in cream and pour over the mould before serving. A small can of truffles is a great improvement. Pour the liquor from the truffles in the meat, slice them and stew one-half to go with the champignons in the hole, the other half with the champignons in the cream. This is nice moulded in individual moulds.

JELLIED CHICKEN

Mrs. Strauder Goff

Cook a large chicken as if for croquettes. After it is cool, take the meat from the bones. Put the skin and the cracked bones back into the broth, which should be about a quart. Add a small onion cut up, 2 bay leaves, a blade of mace, and a pinch of celery seed. Simmer till reduced to a pint. Cut up the meat of the chicken as if for salad or a little finer, and have ready 4 hard-boiled eggs and a little chopped parsley. Dip a mould, melon-shaped ones are pretty, in ice water and arrange the chicken and the eggs, which must be sliced in layers with a little chopped parsley now and then. Strain the broth, season with salt and a tablespoon of sherry wine, and pour over the chicken and set on the ice for several hours or over night. Turn into a dish bordered with lettuce and serve with mayonnaise or French dressing. It may also be served with a row of peeled tomatoes around the mould, or in winter with tomato jelly moulded in small moulds, or the chicken may be moulded in the individual moulds round a large mould of the tomato jelly. Mayonnaise should accompany either arrangement.

PRESSED CHICKEN

E. D. P.

1 chicken,
3 sets of sweetbreads,
1 teacup of cream,
1 onion,
A little parsley,
Salt and pepper to taste,
1 tablespoon of butter.

Boil the chicken till tender, also the sweetbreads. When cold, grind through the meatgrinder. Boil the onion in the cream and season with parsley, salt, and pepper. Thicken with a little flour rubbed in the butter. When it begins to thicken, strain and mix with chicken and sweetbreads. Mould with aspic jelly. This makes 2 moulds.

QUENELLES

E. D. P.

Mix 1 pound of cold turkey or chicken breast with
    6 ounces of panada,
¼ pound of pickled pork,
¼ pound of butter,
½ teacup of cream,

71

Onion, salt, and pepper to taste,
1 lemon.

Shape 3 inches long. Roll in flour and drop in boiling water.

Serve with champignon sauce.

RISSOLES

¼ pound of ground turkey heart,
3 sets of sweetbreads chopped,
¼ pound of butter,
¼ pound of flour,
1 pint of strong veal stock,
3 eggs.

Put the butter in a stew-pan; when it bubbles add the flour; let it cook, but do not let it boil; add the stock, then the turkey and sweetbreads, and when it is thick, add the eggs; cook the whole until it is as stiff as the panada for croquettes. Set it aside to cool, then add enough cream to make it soft, but not too wet. Make fine pastry thick as a biscuit, and cut with a biscuit cutter; then roll it out thin. Put a large spoonful in centre of each, and turn over like a turn-over pie; dip in eggs, roll in vermicelli, and fry a light brown.

CREAMED SWEETBREADS

Mrs. Henry C. Buckner

Take blanched sweetbreads and cut them in small pieces and put in a saucepan with 1 tablespoon of butter rolled in 1 tablespoon of flour, slowly adding 1 pint of cream, and salt and pepper to taste. Serve hot.

If preferred, mushrooms are a nice addition.

FRIED SWEETBREADS WITH PEAS

Stew the breads, but do not cut them up. Make a batter and dip the breads in and fry in hot lard. Cook the peas in salt water and serve with the breads.

HOW TO BLANCH SWEETBREADS

Soak 3 hours in 3 different waters with 1 pinch of salt in each water. Drain, place in cold water, and boil till tender. Throw in cold water to whiten. Put in a cold place, and they are ready for general use.

STEWED SWEETBREADS

V. C. G.

Boil the sweetbreads till tender enough to pick them to pieces, and take out the strings and hard pieces. Then put them on to stew with cream, seasoning with pepper, salt, and a very little mace. Then add a lump of butter with a few bread-crumbs and yolks of 2 eggs beaten light.

Cook till thick as very thin mush. This recipe is for 2 pairs.

SWEETBREADS WITH CHAMPIGNONS

E. D. P.

1 can of champignons,
1 set of sweetbreads,
½ pint of clear soup,
1 teaspoon of flour,
½ teaspoon of brown flour,
½ tablespoon of butter,
1 wineglass of wine,
Salt and pepper to taste.

Cook the sweetbreads thoroughly and cook the champignons with their liquor in a saucepan with the clear soup. Boil nearly an hour; season well, and put sweetbreads in. Add butter and flour. Cook till thick, and add wine last. Serve hot.

SWEETBREADS WITH PEAS

Take the skin and fat off the breads and let them stand in salt water for a few minutes. Cut into pieces and boil till done. Boil the peas in salted water and put with the breads. Take the liquor from the peas and thicken with flour and season highly with pepper, salt, and butter. Cook a few minutes and pour over the dish.

TIMBALE

Mrs. Henry C. Buckner

Boil 6 or 8 large sticks of macaroni, broken in 1-inch lengths, 25 minutes, and put in cold water to bleach; decorate a medium-sized bowl, holding about 3 pints, with pieces of macaroni an inch long. The inside of the bowl is thickly buttered to hold macaroni, and put in close together up to the top of the bowl. The filling is made of the breast of 1 large chicken, raw.

1 large slice of bread, soaked in cream,
¼ pound of butter,

Yolks of 5 eggs,
½ can mushrooms chopped,
A little grated nutmeg,
Salt and pepper to taste,
¼ teaspoon celery seed,
1 pinch of thyme,
⅓ teaspoon fresh onion juice.

All these ingredients are put in a chopping-dish and powdered to a paste or ground in a fine meat-grinder. Put in a mould, tie buttered paper on top and steam nearly 4 hours. Serve with timbale sauce.

TIMBALE SHELLS

Mix ¾ of a cup of flour with ½ teaspoon of salt; add ⅔ cup of milk and 1 egg, well beaten; when very smooth add 1 tablespoon of oil; dip hot timbale iron in this batter and fry the mixture which clings to the iron in hot lard.

XALAPA BOUDINS

Mrs. Henry C. Buckner

Six chicken livers boiled 30 minutes. When cold, pound to a smooth paste and rub through a sieve. Boil 1 pint of cream or chicken stock and

1 cup of stale bread-crumbs until as smooth as paste. Then

> 8 tablespoons of butter,
> The livers,
> 1 tablespoon of salt,
> ½ teaspoon of pepper,
> Dash of red pepper.

When cold, add 3 eggs, beaten very light. Cook in moulds in water at the boiling point, but do not let it boil. When a large mould is used, it will take 1 hour; in the small cups, 40 minutes.

Serve with sauce for Xalapa Boudins.

Croquettes

BRAIN CROQUETTES

Soak the brains 1 hour and parboil them for 5 minutes. Season highly with salt and pepper and a little sage. Add $\frac{1}{3}$ as much cracker-crumbs as brains. Work all together with 2 tablespoons of sweet rich cream, white of an egg, whipped to a froth. Make into shapes, roll them in raw yolk and bread-crumbs and fry pretty brown.

CHICKEN CROQUETTES

Mrs. Ellet Cabell

Take a chicken and wrap in a cloth and boil till tender. Add to the water parsley, salt, and a little onion. Skim the water and set aside to cool. When the chicken is cold, skin and cut up, removing all gristle and fat. Chop and add 2 tablespoons flour and 1 of butter. Take $2\frac{1}{2}$ cups of liquor, season with salt, pepper, and mace, and boil. When it boils, stir in the butter and flour till very smooth. Add 1 large cup of bread-crumbs and mix thoroughly. Add the minced chicken, and cook all for a few minutes and set aside to cool. Mould into croquettes, dip in the beaten egg and then cracker-dust. Let them stand awhile and fry in boiling lard, and drain as soon as done.

VERY FINE CROQUETTES

E. D. P.

1 pound of cooked turkey or chicken,
3 teaspoons of chopped parsley,
1 pint of cream,
1 large onion,
¼ pound of butter,
¼ pound of bread-crumbs,
Salt, pepper, and cayenne pepper to taste.

Sprinkle the parsley over the meat and run through grinder twice. Boil the onion with the cream and strain onion out, and when cool pour cream over bread-crumbs, add the butter, and make a stiff mixture, then add salt, etc. Beat in the meat and mix all together.

If too stiff, add a little cream and make as soft as can be handled. Put on ice to get stiff. Then roll and shape. Dip in egg, and roll in bread-crumbs, and fry in hot lard.

EGG CROQUETTES

Miss Annie White

For 6 croquettes take 6 eggs,
1 pint milk,
1 tablespoon butter,
1 tablespoon flour,
1 tablespoon chopped parsley,
10 drops onion juice,
1 teaspoon salt,
1 teaspoon pepper.

Boil eggs hard and drop in cold water, and, after removing shells, squeeze through potato-masher. Boil the milk, and add the flour and butter, which have been well mixed, then add other ingredients.

Turn in a platter to cool. Let the mixture stand 3 hours. Shape and drop in egg and bread-crumbs and fry in boiling fat.

FISH CROQUETTES

Rub together 3 tablespoons of flour, 1 of butter, stir into ½ pint of rich milk; add a teaspoon of finely chopped parsley, and a quarter of a tea-spoon onion juice. Boil until it thickens; add 2 cups of cold boiled fish, and boil up again; season with salt and pepper to taste. When cold, take out and dip in egg, then in bread-crumbs, and fry.

OYSTER CROQUETTES

Drain 1 quart oysters and chop fine. Take 1 pint bread-crumbs and add 1 teaspoon baking-powder. Mix oysters and crumbs and pour over 1 cup of cream. Season with pepper, salt, and 1 tablespoon butter. Fix well and add 2 well-beaten eggs. Make into shapes and dip in egg, roll in cracker-dust, and fry a rich brown.

RICE CROQUETTES

Mrs. Strauder Goff

1½ pints boiled rice,
3 eggs,
Butter size of 1½ eggs,
3 tablespoons cream,
½ teaspoon scraped onion,
Salt and cayenne pepper to taste,
A small pinch of mace.

Reserve 2 whites of the eggs to roll the croquettes in. Mix the ingredients and cook in a double boiler till quite thick. Allow to cool. Form into croquettes and fry in deep fat, after rolling in the whites of the eggs and bread-crumbs.

The seasoning can be varied by omitting the mace and adding a half a teacup of grated cheese or grated ham, or a cup of chopped chicken or brains. They should always be served with tomato sauce.

SALMON CROQUETTES

1 can salmon,
2 eggs,
$\frac{1}{2}$ cup of butter,
1 cup of fine bread-crumbs,
1 teaspoon baking-powder in bread-crumbs,
$\frac{1}{2}$ cup of cream,
$\frac{1}{4}$ teaspoon of cayenne pepper,
Salt to taste.

Mix all together and make in pear shape. Roll in egg and cracker-dust, and fry light brown.

Fowl

BAKED CHICKEN

Prepare young grown chicken 12 hours or more before using. Place the chicken flat in the pan. Add 1 pint water and cook till tender. Baste often with butter. Then make a dressing of butter, salt, pepper, a little onion and bread-crumbs and put around the chicken. Cook till chicken and dressing are a rich brown.

BROILED CHICKEN

Prepare young chicken, split on the back, sprinkle with salt, and lay on ice 12 hours or longer before it is cooked. Have broiling-irons very hot. Spread a spoon of butter on the chicken, add salt and pepper, and lay on the broiler with the breast next the fire. Cover and put a weight on top— the old-fashioned way was to put a flat-iron on top.

Be careful to broil both sides, basting with a little butter. Cook till tender and a rich brown. Place on dish and pour the liquor from the broiler over it.

CHICKEN PIE

Cut up a large chicken, add sufficient water to make a good gravy. Add $\frac{1}{4}$ pound of butter rolled in flour, little salt, pepper, and mace to taste. Make a paste with $\frac{3}{4}$ pound of flour and $\frac{1}{4}$ pound of butter, little water, and a pinch of salt. Boil 3 eggs hard. Stir the yolks in the pie, and bake.

CHICKEN PUDDING

Stew 3 chickens until tender; remove from the liquor; put into a baking-dish and make a batter with flour, sweet milk, a tablespoon of butter, and 3 eggs beaten separately; beat all thoroughly and pour on the chicken; bake 1 hour; serve with gravy made of the liquor the chicken was boiled in; thicken with flour, add butter, salt, and pepper to taste.

CHICKEN FOR SUPPER

After boiling chickens in as little water as possible until the meat falls from the bones, pick off the meat, chop it rather fine, and season it well with pepper and salt; put into the bottom of a mould some slices of hard-boiled eggs and layers of chicken until mould is nearly full; boil down the water the chicken was boiled in until there is about a cupful left; season it well and pour it over the chicken; it will sink through, forming a jelly around it. Let it stand over night or all day on ice. Let it be sliced at table. Garnish the dish with light-colored celery-leaves or fringed celery.

CURRIED CHICKEN

Boil chicken tender; take out and lay on platter; take 1 teaspoon of curry and flour enough to make the liquor the thickness of good gravy; mix both together smooth with a little water, and stir into liquor the chicken was boiled in; then put back the chicken, and let all boil slowly for 15 minutes, stirring slightly.

FRICASSEE OF CHICKEN
E. D. P.

1 tender chicken,
1 teacupful of butter,
1 tablespoonful of flour,

1 bunch of parsley,
1 saltspoonful of celery seed.

Wash the chicken and cut it up as for frying; put into a stew-pan, with hot water enough to cover it, add the celery seed and salt; let it boil gently, taking off the scum as it rises, until it is tender, which will take about 1 hour; then rub the butter and flour together, put into the stew-pan with the well-chopped parsley; let it stew 15 minutes; add the yolks of 2 raw eggs; stir as you would for custard, and boil 5 minutes longer. Serve on a dish with boiled rice arranged nicely around it. When putting the celery into the stew-pan put it in a thin piece of muslin.

FRIED CHICKEN

Prepare young chicken and sprinkle with salt and lay on ice 12 hours before cooking. Cut the chicken in pieces and dredge with flour and drop in hot boiling lard and butter—equal parts—salt and pepper, and cover tightly and cook rather slowly—if it cooks too quickly it will burn. Cook both sides to a rich brown. Remove chicken and make a gravy by adding milk, flour, butter, salt, and pepper. Cook till thick, and serve in separate bowl.

ROASTED CHICKEN

Prepare a full-grown chicken or hen, sprinkle with salt, lay on ice for 12 hours or longer. Put in pan and add 1 pint water, and cook till tender, adding water if needed. Then make a dressing of bread-crumbs, butter, salt and pepper, and a little onion, and make into cakes and lay around the fowl. Baste frequently with butter. Do not put the stuffing inside the fowl, as it will absorb the juices. Cook the giblets in the pan with the chicken. When the chicken is tender and cakes are a rich brown, remove from the pan. To the giblets add flour, butter, a little milk, and make a gravy, which serve in a separate bowl.

STEWED CHICKEN

Three young chickens cut up and laid in salt and water; drain the water; wipe and flour the chickens. Add ¼ pound of butter, half an onion, salt and pepper, a blade of mace. Cover close and stew till tender.

Put in the gravy the yolks of 2 eggs, beaten, ½ pint of cream, and a little lemon-juice.

89

CHICKEN TERRAPIN

E. D. P.

Cut a cold boiled chicken and liver in small pieces. Remove skin, fat, and gristle. Put in a pan with

½ pint of cream,

¼ pound of butter, rolled in 1 tablespoon of flour,

Salt to taste.

Chop up 3 hard-boiled eggs. Add eggs and when it comes to a boil stir in a wineglass of sherry.

BOILED FOWL WITH OYSTERS

Take a young chicken, fill the inside with oysters, and put it into a jar, and plunge the jar into a kettle of water, remembering to cover tightly; boil for 1½ hours; there will be a quantity of gravy from the juice of the fowl and the oysters in the jar, which make into a white sauce with the addition of a little flour, cream, and butter; add some oysters to it or serve plain with the chicken. The gravy that comes from a fowl dressed in this manner will be a stiff jelly next day, and the fowl will be white and tender and of an exceedingly fine flavor—advantages not attained in ordinary boiling—while the dish loses nothing of its delicacy and simplicity.

BROILED DUCK

Take young, tender ducks (after they are feathered), and broil according to recipe for broiled chicken.

ROAST DUCK

Sprinkle well with salt and pepper, and fill the duck with a dressing made of bread-crumbs, butter, salt and pepper, and a little onion.

Place 2 slices of pork across breast and put in roaster. Add hot water, and baste frequently. Serve with gravy and currant jelly.

ROAST GOOSE

Sprinkle with salt and pepper and put the goose in a roaster, and add water and baste frequently. Make a dressing of bread-crumbs, sage, butter, onion, salt and pepper, and mix together with an egg.

Stuff the goose and cook for 2 hours. Make a gravy. Serve with apple-sauce.

BROILED TURKEY

Take young turkeys, about 4 months old, and broil as you would any young fowl.

ROASTED TURKEY

A turkey should be killed and dressed from two days to a week before cooking. Rub thoroughly the breast and back with salt and pepper and lay in the roasting pan with the breast down. Place the giblets in the pan and fill with water to the depth of 2 inches. Have the oven hot and keep the heat even. Baste often. A young, tender turkey can be cooked in 2 hours, but an older one requires a longer time—3 or 4 hours may be necessary. When the turkey is done, having tested it by sticking a fork in the breast, turn it over on its back and brown the breast. Make a dressing of bread-crumbs, season with salt and pepper, a little onion, or sage if preferred. Place the dressing around the turkey when it is half done, and brown nicely.

Game

BLUE GRASS RECIPE FOR ROAST QUAIL

E. D. P.

Rub the quail inside with pepper and put a slice of pickled pork on breast-bone of each, with salt and pepper. Baste often, and fill, when half done, with chestnut dressing as for turkey.

BROILED PARTRIDGES

Open on back; if partridges are not tender, place in a small baking-pan with $\frac{1}{2}$ inch hot water, and cover; 15 minutes is long enough if the oven is hot; dredge well with flour; lay on broiling-irons, breast down; make gravy of two tablespoons of flour in $\frac{1}{2}$ cup of cold water, with pepper, salt, and butter; stir this into liquid in which birds are parboiled; always serve with toast and bacon, if

93

preferred with this gravy. Slash birds in breast three times when done; put a little butter in each slash, also pepper and salt; place on toast, then pour liquor from pan over them.

BROILED PHEASANT

If the pheasant is young, broil as you would young chicken. If full grown, cut into pieces, after having parboiled it, and add butter, salt, and pepper, and broil over a hot fire. Serve on thin slices of toast.

BROILED SQUIRREL

If young and tender, broil as you would young chicken. If old, bake as you would chicken.

QUAIL WITH TRUFFLES

E. D. P.

Broil delicately the breast of the quail, and cook truffles for $\frac{3}{4}$ hour in 1 pint of clear soup. Thicken with browned flour and 1 tablespoon of butter. Add wine to taste. Place quail's breast on dish. Scatter the truffles over it and pour the sauce over.

ROASTED PHEASANT

Roast as you would a chicken, and serve hot.

RABBIT ROASTED

Skin and dress the rabbit, cutting off the head and tail. Stuff with dressing of bread-crumbs, salt and pepper. Put in pan with water, and bake as you would chicken. Baste often with butter. Serve with apple-sauce and rice-cakes.

ROASTED VENISON

Rub the meat well with salt and pepper and lay in a double baking-pan and add 1 quart of water. Let it cook till it is tender, about $2\frac{1}{2}$ or 3 hours. Make a dressing of bread-crumbs, salt and pepper and put around the meat. Sprinkle bread-crumbs thickly over the top with bits of butter and a little pepper. Baste often and cook to a nice brown. Thicken the gravy with flour and serve in a gravy boat. Serve with currant jelly.

Meats

BAKED HAM

Never bake a ham under a year old. Rub the ham thoroughly and put to soak in cold water for 24 hours. Then cover with cold water in a boiler. When it begins to boil, set on back of stove and boil slowly till the bone is loose. (Twenty minutes to a pound is about the length of time required.) Then remove from stove and let stand in boiler till it is cool, over night or half a day. Put in a baking-pan and remove the skin and extra fat, being careful to keep the shape. Make a stiff batter of flour and water and cover the top. Set it in the oven and bake slowly for 2 hours. Then remove batter and with a knife make slight incisions all over the ham and sprinkle first with brown sugar, about 1 tablespoonful, then sprinkle thoroughly with black pepper. Make a dressing of

97

grated bread or crackers, a little onion chopped fine, 1 tablespoon butter, pepper, salt, and mix with 1 egg and a little water. Cover the top with this dressing and put in oven to brown. Serve cold.

COL. WM. RHODES ESTILL'S RECIPE FOR CURING HAMS

Kill your hogs when the wind is from the northwest. The night before you salt the meat take a string of red pepper and make a strong tea. (Let it remain on the stove over night.) Put in the tea 2 heaping tablespoons of saltpetre to every 2 gallons. Take this strong tea and pour on the salt. Salt the meat lightly the first time to run off the blood. Let the meat lie packed 3 days—longer, if the weather is very cold. Then overhaul the meat and put 1 teaspoon of pulverized saltpetre on the flesh side of each ham and rub in well. Then rub with molasses mixed with salt. Pack close for 10 days. After this overhaul again, rubbing each piece, and pack close again. Hang the meat in 3 weeks from the time the hogs were killed. Before hanging, wash each piece in warm water, and while wet roll in hickory ashes. Then smoke with green hickory wood, and tie up in cotton bags in February.

CURING HAMS AT AUVERGNE, PARIS, KY.

HAM COOKED IN WINE

Mrs. Henry C. Buckner

Scrub well and soak an old ham in plenty of water for 48 hours. Weigh ham and allow ½ hour for each pound, place in large ham boiler and fill with cold water; let simmer (not boil) gently the allotted time. When half the time is up, pour off the water; fill again with fresh boiling water, into which put ½ cup of vinegar, a bay leaf and a few cloves, and finish cooking. Let the ham remain in the water until cool. Then remove the skin. Mix 2 tablespoonfuls of "Coleman's Mustard" with vinegar, spread over the ham, brush with the yolk of an egg. Sprinkle with bread-crumbs and sugar, pin on the fat side with cloves and a few raisins.

With a sharp knife make incisions all through the ham, holding back the openings and pouring in ½ pint of sherry. Place in the oven for ⅓ hour, basting every 5 minutes. Do not cut until perfectly cold.

KENTUCKY BAKED HAM

E. D. P.

Take a good magnolia ham 1 or 2 years old and let it soak 36 hours. Make a stiff dough of flour and water and envelop the ham and put in a baking-pan. Add enough water to keep from sticking. Baste frequently and cook till thoroughly done, or till the hock can be removed—5 or 6 hours.

When done, skin it and make an icing of brown sugar and yolk of 1 egg, and cover top and grate bread-crumbs over. Put in oven and brown.

SUGAR-CURED HAMS

Mrs. Cassius M. Clay

Let the hams lie in dry salt for 4 weeks after the killing. Then hang them up in the smoke-house and smoke them with dry hickory chips till they are a pretty light brown. Then rub them thoroughly with a pomatum made of New Orleans molasses, black and red pepper, using about 3 times as much black pepper as red. Mix the molasses and pepper in a large dish-pan, and if they do not mix easily, warm them by setting the pan on the stove. When it is well mixed, have a man hold the ham by the hock with one hand, and with the other rub the mixture well into the ham on both sides. Make good strong sacks and tie each ham and hang up with the hock down, as the ingredients will be absorbed more readily.

They will be ready for use in about 8 or 10 months.

Hams a year old are better than older hams, as they get too dry and strong when kept too long. In cooking the ham a handful of cloves dropped in the water while boiling gives it a rich flavor.

BAKED HASH

E. D. P.

Run any kind of cold cooked meat through the grinder. Equal parts of mashed Irish potatoes. Salt and pepper to taste. Butter and milk enough to keep it from being too stiff. Put in a baking-dish and pour over 2 tablespoons of tomato catsup. Sprinkle well with bread-crumbs and brown. Serve hot.

BEEF À LA MODE (No. 1)

Mrs. Brutus J. Clay

Take a round of beef and remove the bone. Fill the hole with a dressing made of bread-crumbs, salt, pepper, and butter. Also 1 teaspoon salt, pepper, cloves, mace, and nutmeg. Make incisions in the beef and put in strips of pork which

101

have been rolled in the spices. Sprinkle the rest over the top. Then cover the whole with fat bacon to prevent burning. Tie with a tape and skewer it well and put in an oven and bake 5 hours. Baste constantly with butter and lard mixed with a little flour. When nearly done skim off the fat and thicken the gravy. Season with walnut catsup and wine.

BEEF À LA MODE (No. 2)

R. V. J.

Take a large tender round of beef and have holes made all over it, through and through. Make a rich stuffing of bread-crumbs, butter, onion, spices, salt, and herbs to your taste; also truffles and mushrooms. If you use the latter, leave out the onion.

Fill the holes with the stuffing, pouring in wine with it into each hole, and then pour more wine over the beef, and let stand until morning. Then bake *slowly* until *thoroughly* done, basting frequently with the wine gravy.

BROILED STEAK

Pepper a nice beefsteak and put on broiler over clear coals. Broil half done, and turn the other side. Have dish hot with butter, salt, and pepper mixed. Turn the steak in this mixture and return to fire, and broil a little longer. Return to dish, turn again, and serve hot.

BROILED VENISON

E. D. P.

Take nicely cut steaks and broil over hot coals. Remove and rub with butter. Broil a few minutes longer and place on a hot dish. Melt currant jelly and season with wine. Add a little more butter to hot steaks and pour wine and jelly over.

Omit jelly and wine and serve as you would beefsteak, and serve with thin slices of lemon.

FRIED FROGS' LEGS

Boil in salt water for 3 minutes. Beat

> 2 eggs,
> 1 cup of milk, and
> Salt and pepper,

and dip first in egg, then in cracker-dust. Put in frying-basket. Dip in skillet of boiling lard and fry rich brown and serve at once.

FRIED PIGS' FEET

Mix well-beaten eggs with salt and pepper and dip the pigs' feet in it, then in the bread-crumbs, and let the egg dry. Fry in skillet of hot lard till a rich brown.

HAMBURG STEAK

Miss Elise White

2 pounds lean meat,
2 teaspoons salt,
1 teaspoon pepper,
1 tablespoon onion juice.

Run the meat through a meat-chopper twice and add the seasoning and shape like a steak and broil. Serve hot with butter.

To get onion juice. Peel an onion and cut in pieces and squeeze through lemon squeezer.

HENRY CLAY'S FAVORITE DISH

Mrs. Henry Clay

Have the butcher extract the bone from the rump roast and take a few stitches with his needle to keep it in good shape. Place the beef in an iron pot with a tight cover; put with it 2 small onions, 2 cloves stuck in each, a pod of red pepper, salt, a little allspice, and 2 carrots. Pour enough boiling water over the beef to nearly cover it; let it come to a hard boil, then set it back, tightly covered, to where it will just simmer for 6 hours. Then place the beef on a hot platter, strain its liquor, and skim every particle of grease from it. Have ready $\frac{1}{2}$ teaspoon of sugar, browned in an iron pan, pour the liquor over it and thicken with a little flour and water. Pour the gravy, which should be quite brown and thick, over the beef. Slice the carrots, which place on and around the beef.

LAMB CHOPS

The chops should be trimmed nicely and peppered well and rolled in butter. Broil nicely on both sides over clear fire. When done, put butter, pepper, and salt over them.

Cover the ends with little white fluted papers and serve on dish with peas.

LOBSTER OR SALMON CHOPS

Miss Virginia Croxton

Boil in salt water for 20 to 25 minutes. Chop as fine as possible.

> ½ pint sweet cream,
> Butter size of an egg

Peel and chop 1 onion into cream. Add 1 tablespoon of cornstarch wet with the cold cream.

Boil and stir in the lobster or salmon, season with cayenne and a little Worcestershire sauce. When cold, form into chop shape, dip in the beaten yolk of an egg, then in the bread or cracker-crumbs, and fry in hot lard as you would oysters. If canned lobsters or salmon is used, omit the boiling. One can makes a good dish.

MEAT CAKES FOR BREAK-FAST

Take any cold meat, except ham, and put through a meat-grinder. Mix with bread-crumbs, a little onion, ½ cup of crumbs, ½ cup of meat, 1 egg, butter, salt, and pepper to taste.

Make in cakes and fry a light brown in butter. Serve with a sauce of milk, flour, butter, salt, and pepper boiled thick.

SADDLE OF MUTTON

Mrs. Henry C. Buckner

Wash it in soda water. Wipe dry, and then rub with soda, brown sugar, cayenne pepper, and salt. Grate a nutmeg over it. Make a dressing of

> Bread-crumbs,
> Brown sugar,
> Chopped celery,
> Tablespoon of butter,
> Salt and pepper,
> Teaspoon of powdered allspice.

Cook from 4 to 5 hours, according to size. Make a gravy of

> 1 pint of brown flour,
> 1 tumbler of brown sugar,
> 2 lemons,
> 1 teaspoon of allspice,
> 1 nutmeg,
> 1 tumbler of jelly,
> ½ teacup of butter,
> Chopped celery,
> Salt and pepper.

ROAST MUTTON

Allow 15 minutes to the pound in roasting mutton. Baste often and serve with jelly.

ROAST BEEF (No. 1)

Select a nice sirloin of beef and place in pan with beef drippings. Beef requires 15 minutes to the pound for cooking. Baste well. When nearly done, sprinkle with salt and pepper and a little flour.

When well cooked to a nice brown, remove from fire and make a gravy by adding a little hot water and thickening. Serve in separate bowl.

ROAST BEEF (No. 2)

Mrs. Mary Webb

Get a choice roast, and after cooking a little while in plenty of water, season with salt and pepper, then pour most of the water from the pan and add the juice from 1 quart of tomatoes.

To the tomatoes add

> 2 teaspoons ground allspice,
> 1 teaspoon cloves,
> 1 teaspoon black pepper,

108

2 teaspoons salt,
A little red pepper,
Small piece of butter,
Small onion chopped fine.

Cook this a few minutes and spread over the roast. Continue basting till done. Add hot water if dressing is too thick.

ROAST PIG

E. D. P.

1 young pig,
2 onions,
1 cup of bread-crumbs,
2 teaspoons of summer savory,
2 tablespoons of butter,
1 saltspoon of salt,
1 egg,
Black pepper to taste.

Make a dressing of butter and bread-crumbs. Add the eggs, chopped onion, and seasoning, and let it simmer. Clean pig well and stuff with dressing and sew up. Rub pig with butter, sprinkle salt and pepper, and dredge with flour. Cut the skin in squares and put in roasting-pan and pour hot water in pan. Roast in moderate oven, basting often, and cook 3½ hours. Make a gravy of the drippings, a little seasoning, and thicken with flour.

Decorate the pig with an apple or sweet potato in the mouth. Have the pig kneel in a bank of green parsley or watercress.

SAUSAGE MEAT
E. D. P.

11 pounds of tender lean pork,
7 pounds of leaf fat,
5 tablespoonsful of powdered sage,
4 teaspoonsful of salt,
3 tablespoons of ground black pepper,
1 level teaspoonful cayenne pepper.

Run all through the grinder twice and then mix well with the hands.

SCRAPPLE

Clean a pig's head nicely and boil till meat leaves bones, and when cold remove grease and chop meat into small pieces. Heat the meat and liquor again, and stir corn meal in gradually till it is thick as mush. Season highly with pepper, salt, and sage. Mould in pans, and when cold slice thin, roll in meal, and fry in hot lard.

SPICED BEEF ROUND

To a round weighing 8 or 10 pounds allow 2 gallons of water. Put into a large vessel to boil; add 4 onions, 1 pint of strong vinegar, 1 teacup of sugar, salt to taste, 2 teaspoons of black pepper, 1 teaspoon of celery seed, 1 teaspoon of ground allspice, a few cloves, 1 thyme, 1 slice of pork, 1 teacup of green tomato catsup, 1 glass of jelly, 1 glass of wine; the wine and jelly can be omitted. Boil 4 hours until the bone becomes loose in the round; then take up the beef and remove the bone, having ready stuffing made either of old biscuit or light bread soaked in the gravy the beef was cooked in; mash fine and fill the opening left by the beef bone; also fill in all spaces and cut places; then wrap in a clean white cloth and tie; press into a pan and put a weight on it, and set aside to get cold. When ready to use, remove the cloth and put the moulded beef in a dish. Cut in thin slices across the top with a sharp knife. Serve with the gravy, which should be boiled down, after taking the meat out, and thickened with brown flour. The gravy should be warmed over when used. In cold weather this will keep for three weeks.

STEWED TONGUE

Parboil a fresh tongue and remove the skin; put in water and stew till done. Add 1 onion, allspice, cloves, and pepper; stew about 3 hours. Before serving add a lump of butter sufficient to season it, together with catsups of all kinds. Nice for tea, and is also good when cold.

TERRAPIN

E. D. P.

Dress carefully 3 small terrapins, and cook till well done, an hour or longer, or less, if tender.

Take the yolks of 3 hard-boiled eggs and mix with ¼ pound of butter. Put in sauce-pan with the terrapin and a teacup of cream and dissolve all well. Then season with pepper and salt and ½ cup of sherry or Madeira wine. Garnish with thin slices of lemon.

HOW TO OPEN TERRAPIN

E. D. P.

Place on back with feet to you. Remove the gall-bladder carefully from left-hand liver. The other liver may be cut up. Leave out nails and bones of head. Put the eggs in cold water after removing film around them.

HOW TO DRESS TERRAPIN

E. D. P.

Throw the terrapin in boiling water. Remove and boil in fresh water. Rub the terrapin with a towel to remove outside skin. Put back in water and boil.

It is cooked when the joints of the leg break easily.

HOW TO CORN BEEF

E. D. P.

4 gallons of water,
5 pounds of salt,
2 ounces of saltpetre,
1½ pounds of brown sugar.

Mix the above and boil 15 minutes, and skim well. The meat must have been rubbed well in salt and saltpetre, and packed for 3 days before. When mixture is cold, pour over meat and let it stand a week. This is excellent for tongues.

HOW TO BOIL CORNED BEEF

1 piece of corned beef,
6 cloves (whole),
6 allspice (whole).

Soak for $\frac{1}{2}$ hour in cold water. Then pour off and cover with fresh water. When it begins to boil, set back on range and add spices and let it simmer for 4 or 5 hours, skimming well. When done, put in small vessel. Put a plate on top and press down with heavy flat-iron. Let stand till next day.

VEAL LOAF

E. D. P.

2 pounds of lean veal,
Large slice of raw ham or
$\frac{1}{4}$ of pickled pork,
3 teaspoons of parsley chopped very fine,
$\frac{1}{2}$ teaspoon of onion chopped very fine,
Salt, pepper, and cayenne pepper to taste,
$\frac{1}{4}$ pound of butter,
3 eggs.

Run the meat and onions (three small-sized ones) through the grinder twice till very smooth. Cream all this with $\frac{1}{4}$ pound of butter and break in the

eggs one at a time. Beat this mixture until light.
Shape into loaf and bake for 3 hours. Sprinkle
with grated bread-crumbs. Put some water in the
pan and skim off the grease and thicken the gravy
with brown flour. This is delicious for tea or to
take on a picnic.

VENISON

Mrs. C. S. Brent

Put the venison to bake. Make a dressing of
bread-crumbs highly seasoned with salt and pepper.
When the meat is half done, turn it over and cut
on either side places $2\frac{1}{2}$ inches long, which fill with
the dressing. Pour over the meat $\frac{1}{2}$ cup of catsup.
Take $\frac{1}{2}$ cup black molasses, 1 tablespoon allspice, and 1 tablespoon brown sugar. Put this too
over the meat. Then crumble the light bread over.
Baste often, for it burns easily. Just before removing from the fire put bits of currant jelly here
and there.

Sauces for Entrées, Fish, Fowl and Meats

AGRA DOLCE

Mrs. Henry C. Buckner

Mix together

2 heaping tablespoonfuls of brown sugar,
¼ bar of grated chocolate,
1 tablespoonful each of shredded candied orange
    and lemon peel,
10 blanched almonds, cut,
½ cupful of currants,
1 cupful of vinegar.

Let them soak for 2 hours, then pour over the cooked meat and simmer for 10 minutes.

Nice for mutton, venison, sweetbreads, calf's head, etc.

A GOOD SAUCE FOR COLD MEATS AND FISH

Mrs. Henry C. Buckner

Yolks of 4 eggs,
½ teaspoonful of salt,
Dash of cayenne pepper,
4 tablespoonfuls of salad oil,
1 tablespoonful of hot water,
1 tablespoonful of tarragon vinegar.

Beat the yolks, add the oil and water. Stand the bowl in boiling water till it thickens. Remove and add salt, pepper, and vinegar. It should be creamy and of the consistency of mayonnaise. A few chopped capers, olives, and cucumbers make it a good Tartare sauce, and a little tomato purée will make it a red sauce for fish.

APPLE SAUCE FOR DUCK

Pare 12 apples and cover with small quantity of water and cook till tender. Strain through a colander and add ½ cup of sugar.

CAPER SAUCE

The yolks of two eggs,
½ cup of olive oil,

3 tablespoons of vinegar,
1 of mustard,
1 teaspoon of sugar,
¼ teaspoon of red pepper,
1 teaspoon of salt,
1 teaspoon of onion juice,
1 tablespoon of chopped capers,
1 tablespoon of chopped cucumber pickles.

Make the same as mayonnaise dressing, add the chopped things last. This sauce can be used with fish and boiled meats, or meats served in jelly.

CELERY SAUCE

Take cream or rich milk, and boil with pieces of celery till the flavor is extracted. Remove it and season sauce with salt and pepper, and add butter, then a little flour to thicken it.

Serve with vegetables.

CHAMPIGNON SAUCE FOR BOUDINS

Cut up 1 can of champignons and let them boil ½ hour. Add half can of truffles, cut up and boil with champignons, cayenne pepper and salt to taste. As the champignons are salty, do not put too much. Add 1 pint of rich cream, and while

119

boiling, add 1 tablespoon of butter with a little flour to thicken the sauce.

Pour over Boudins and serve.

CHAMPIGNON SAUCE FOR QUENELLES

E. D. P.

2 cans of champignons,
1 quart of clear soup,
1 dessertspoon of flour,
1 large spoon of butter,
2 tablespoons of wine,
Salt and cayenne pepper to taste.

Cut the champignons into small pieces and cook in their own liquor for ½ hour. Let the clear soup come to a boil and add the champignons with the salt and pepper. Rub flour and butter together and stir in the champignons until thick as cream.

Heat the wine and pour in just before serving.

CHESTNUT STUFFING FOR TURKEY

E. D. P.

1 teacup of mashed sweet potatoes,
1 teacup of mashed and boiled chestnuts,

AUNT MARIA, COOK AT MOUNT AIRY, PARIS, KY.

1 dessertspoon of butter,
1 wineglass of cream,
Salt and black pepper to the taste.

Mix potatoes, chestnuts, cream, and season. Put stuffing in when turkey is half-roasted. Baste often.

CRANBERRY SAUCE FOR TURKEY

Wash 1 quart of berries. Cover with water in a porcelain kettle and cook till the skins burst. Mash and strain through a colander and return to fire. Add 1 cup of sugar and cook till thick. Mould in any shape and serve cold.

CUCUMBER SAUCE

Mrs. Cyrus McCormick

1 dozen fresh green cucumbers,
1 dozen white onions,
1 quart of good cider vinegar.

Peel and grate the cucumbers and onions and place in a sieve to drain. Place the pulp in a bowl and add black and cayenne pepper and salt to taste and 1 quart or more of good vinegar.

121

Put in wide-mouthed bottles or little glass jars and put 1 tablespoon of olive oil in each before sealing.

This recipe requires no cooking, and will keep 2 years in a cool place.

DRAWN BUTTER FOR FOWL

Melt ¼ pound butter and stir in 2 teaspoons flour. Mix thoroughly and add 6 teaspoons of cold water, a little at a time. Cook till smooth. Add salt and pepper to taste. If preferred, add oysters while mixture is simmering.

FISH SAUCE (No. 1)

V. C. G.

1 pint of boiled milk,
2 tablespoons of butter,
1 tablespoon of flour,
1 tablespoon of wine,
1 tablespoon of capers,
1 egg,
Salt and cayenne pepper to taste.

Put the milk in a saucepan, and when it comes to a boil stir in a well-beaten egg, salt and pepper.

Cream the flour and butter till perfectly smooth, and stir into the milk until it thickens.

Have the capers in the sauce-dish and pour the sauce over them. Serve hot.

FISH SAUCE (No. 2)

V. C. G.

Make mayonnaise of yolks of 2 eggs and oil. Add 1 teaspoon of Worcestershire sauce, 1 grated onion, salt and pepper, and 1 tablespoon of lemon juice, chopped parsley, and pinch of cayenne pepper.

HOLLANDAISE SAUCE

St. Nicholas Hotel

Melt slowly ½ pound of best butter. Put 5 yolks of eggs in a saucepan with a lump of butter the size of an English walnut. Stir briskly with an egg-beater on medium hot place on range. Add a little melted butter, and as soon as it thickens, add gradually more melted butter (like oil for mayonnaise) till the half pound is used. The sauce should be thick. Season to taste, and add a few drops of lemon juice.

HORSERADISH SAUCE

4 tablespoons of grated horseradish,
1 teaspoon of sugar,
1 teaspoon of salt,
½ teaspoon of pepper,
2 teaspoons of mixed mustard and vinegar,
3 or 4 tablespoons of cream.

To serve with hot beef. Put in a jar, which place in a saucepan of boiling hot water.

Do not allow it to boil, or it will curdle.

MINT SAUCE

Mrs. Henry C. Buckner

Put 4 tablespoonfuls of chopped mint,
2 tablespoonfuls of sugar,
¼ pint of vinegar,

into the sauce-boat. Let it remain an hour or two before serving.

MUSTARD SAUCE FOR COLD MEATS

4 tablespoons mustard,
1 tablespoon of sugar,
1 teaspoon each of salt and pepper.

124

Mix with boiling water to consistency of thick paste and thin with vinegar.

OYSTER SAUCE FOR TURKEY

E. D. P.

1 quart of oysters,
1 pint of cream, or rich milk,
1 dessertspoon of flour,
Salt and pepper to the taste.

Strain the liquor and put in a saucepan to boil. Add the cream, then the flour, moistening with a little cold water. Let this boil till thick, then season and drop the oysters in. When they curl, take them off and serve in sauce-boat.

If milk is used, put in extra teaspoon of flour and a large spoon of butter.

SAUCE FOR CROQUETTES

Mrs. B. F. Buckner

Make a thick cream gravy of 1 teacup of tomato catsup and 1 tablespoon of Worcestershire sauce. Serve hot with croquettes.

SAUCE FOR MEATS

1 teacup of grated horseradish,
1 wineglass of good vinegar,
1 dessertspoon of sugar,
1 dessertspoon of mustard,
1 teaspoon of salt,
Mix well and serve on meat.

SAUCE FOR QUENELLES

E. D. P.

2 cans of champignons,
1 pint of cream,
1 heaping tablespoon of butter,
1 tablespoon of flour,
Nutmeg, salt, and cayenne pepper to taste.

Cut champignons in small pieces and put in saucepan with their own liquor and cook for one-half hour. Stir in cream. Rub flour and butter together and add gradually. Boil 5 minutes and season highly.

Use 2 tablespoons of this sauce for the quenelles, leaving out the champignons.

SAUCE RÉMOLADE

Given Mrs. W. W. Massie at Hotel Belle Vue,
Munich

Put the yolks of 4 eggs in a bowl with ½ teaspoon each of salt and pepper. Beat in olive oil until it thickens; then pour in 3 tablespoons tarragon vinegar and oil alternately until half a litre (½ pt.) of oil has been used. Chop fine

5 eschalots (a kind of onion),
1 tablespoon of capers,
5 small cucumber pickles,
A little tarragon and spinach.

Beat them together with 1 tablespoon of mustard into the prepared sauce. Add the juice of ½ lemon and a little cayenne pepper, as this sauce should be piquant.

Excellent for cold chicken or meats.

SAUCE FOR XALAPA BOUDINS

Yolks of 3 eggs. Place bowl over top of teakettle and stir till it begins to thicken. Then add teaspoon of butter; stir until melted. Stir in 6 more teaspoons of butter the same way. Then add ½ pint of cream, little by little, till all is used.

TARTARE SAUCE FOR FISH

E. D. P.

The yolks of 2 hard-boiled eggs,
The yolks of 2 raw eggs,
8 tablespoonfuls of olive oil,
3 dessertspoonfuls of vinegar,
1 teaspoonful of chopped onion,
1 tablespoonful of capers,
Salt and cayenne pepper to the taste.

Mash the hard-boiled eggs; add the raw eggs to them, and beat until perfectly smooth and light. Then beat in well the oil and vinegar alternately. Add the onion and capers; lastly the salt and cayenne pepper. Serve cold in a sauce-boat.

TIMBALE SAUCE

1 pint cream,
1 heaping tablespoon of butter,
$\frac{1}{2}$ can mushrooms chopped,
1 tablespoon flour.

Rub the butter and flour together and add the cream slowly; add the mushrooms; season highly with paprika and salt; boil till thick, stirring all the time; serve very hot.

TOMATO SAUCE
(For Steaks and Chops)

V. C. G.

1 pint of tomatoes,
1 small carrot,
2 whole cloves,
3 small pieces of mace,
1 onion,
Salt and pepper to taste.

Put the tomatoes, carrots, and onions in a saucepan, and stew till carrots and onions are tender. Then put them through a sieve, and return to the saucepan, and thicken with a teaspoon of flour and dessertspoon of butter worked together.

Serve hot.

TOMATO SAUCE FOR RICE CROQUETTES

Half a can of tomatoes, put in a saucepan and add a small onion cut up, salt and cayenne pepper, a bay-leaf and a pinch of celery seed. After boiling a few minutes, long enough for the tomato to soften and for the juice to absorb the seasoning, strain, add a dessertspoon of brown sugar and the same of butter with two dessertspoons of flour worked into it. Set back on the stove, and cook till about like cream. Serve hot.

TRUFFLE SAUCE
E. D. P.

1 pound can of truffles,
1 pint of clear soup,
1 tablespoon of butter,
1 teaspoon of white flour,
1 teaspoon of browned flour,
2 tablespoons of sherry wine,
Salt and pepper to the taste.

Chop the truffles and put them with their liquor into a saucepan with the soup. Boil steadily for ½ hour. Rub flour and butter together, stir in truffles, and simmer till thick; then add wine, salt, and cayenne pepper.

Delicious for meats or entrées.

VENISON SAUCE

½ pound brown sugar,
½ pound butter,
½ pint currant jelly,
½ pint claret wine,
1 tablespoon ground mace and cinnamon.
Boil well.

WHITE SAUCE
FOR CREME DE VOLAILLE

1 heaping teaspoon of flour,
2 tablespoons of butter,
1 pint of milk.

Parboil the mushrooms, either 1½ or 2½ cans, as you prefer, and add them to the sauce a few minutes before you take it from the fire. Add a little white pepper to the mushrooms.

WINE SAUCE FOR MUTTON
V. C. G.

1 tumbler of currant jelly,
1 tumbler of tomato catsup,
1 teacup of brown sugar,
1 tumbler of wine,
1 wineglass of brandy,
½ pint of mutton gravy, from which the grease has been skimmed.
Thicken a little with flour.

Vegetables

ASPARAGUS

Tie the asparagus in bunches and boil in salted water till tender. Drain, untie and place on toasted bread. Make a sauce of cream, butter, salt, pepper, a little flour, and boil a few minutes and pour over the asparagus.

BAKED BEANS

Put 1 pint of dry beans and 1 quart of water to soak over night. Wash well and add 3 pints of water and boil till tender, about 2½ hours. Drain off the water and put in baking dish, season with salt, pepper, 2 tablespoons molasses or brown sugar, and lay a few slices of thin bacon on the top. Bake for an hour till a rich brown. Serve warm or cold with tomato catsup.

LIMA BEANS

Shell and wash 1 quart of lima beans and cook in salt water till tender. Drain and add 2 ounces butter, a cup of cream, with salt and pepper to taste.

STRING BEANS

2 quarts beans.

String carefully and put in a saucepan and boil 20 minutes. Drain the water from them and replace with 2 quarts boiling water. Add a piece of bacon or middling and boil 1½ hours.

Instead of the bacon a dressing of 1 pint of cream, a lump of butter, a little flour, salt, and pepper may be used. Serve hot.

BAKED CABBAGE

Take one head of cabbage and remove the outside leaves and split in four sections. Boil in salt water till tender. Drain through a colander. Put in a baking dish and pour over it 1 cup of cream. Add a small piece of butter, with salt and pepper to taste. Break an egg over the centre. Put in oven and bake till brown. Serve hot.

BAKED CAULIFLOWER

E. D. P.

1 fresh cauliflower,
1 ounce of grated Parmesan cheese,
1 ounce of cracker powder,
1 tablespoon of butter,
1 dessertspoon of flour,
White pepper and salt to taste.

Put cauliflower, top down, in salt and water, and let it stand for 1 hour. Put in pot of salted boiling water and boil 20 minutes. Mix butter and flour and add to boiling water, and stir till it thickens. Add salt and pepper. Put cauliflower in baking dish, pour sauce over it, and sprinkle with cheese and cracker-powder. Brown and serve hot.

BOILED CAULIFLOWER

Cut off the stems, pick off the outer leaves, and wash well in cold water and soak for an hour. Then tie the cauliflower in a thin bag and boil for half an hour. When tender lift from the water, remove the cloth and serve with a sauce made of cream, a little flour, butter, salt, and pepper.

BLUE GRASS CORN PUDDING

8 ears of corn,
1 tablespoon of butter,
1 teacup of milk,
1 teaspoon of flour,
Salt and pepper to taste,
3 eggs.

Grate the corn and scrape cob with a knife. Beat the eggs light and stir in cream, butter, and flour, and mix with the milk and add the corn. Season and bake ¾ of an hour.

Mrs. TALBOT'S CORN PUDDING

1 dozen ears of sweet corn,
1 quart of new milk (or use ½ milk and cream),
2 tablespoons of butter,
1 tablespoon of sugar,
1 teaspoon of salt.

Split the corn and scrape well with a knife. Stir in the milk. Break butter into pieces and scatter on top. Add the sugar and stir all well. Cook ½ hour in a hot oven, stirring every 5 minutes until nearly done, then let the top brown.

136

CORN FRITTERS (No. 1)

Mrs. Henry C. Buckner

Beat 2 eggs without separating,
1 cup milk,
1 pint canned corn.

Little salt, sugar, and enough flour for thick batter; add 1 teaspoonful of baking-powder to flour; 1 tablespoon butter; fry in hot lard.

CORN FRITTERS (No. 2)

2 eggs,
1 teacup of new milk,
2 tablespoons butter,
2 tablespoons flour,
1 quart grated corn.

Mix thoroughly and drop with a spoon in hot butter and lard mixed, and fry a rich brown. Salt and pepper to taste.

BAKED EGG-PLANT

Do not peel the plant, but parboil it till tender, and then throw it into cold water. Then peel and cut it open and remove the seed and fill with a dressing made of bread-crumbs, a little chopped

137

onion, butter, salt, and pepper. Put in a pan with a little water and bake a rich brown.

FRIED EGG-PLANT

After peeling the plant cut in slices and lay in salt water. Steam till tender. Make a batter of

2 eggs beaten separately,
1 teacup of sour cream,
1 teaspoon salt,
½ teaspoon soda,
Flour enough to thicken.

Dip the egg plant in the batter and fry a rich brown. Serve hot.

EGG-PLANT PUDDING

E. D. P.

2 egg-plants,
Yolks of 6 hard-boiled eggs,
¼ pound of butter,
1 teaspoon of chopped onion,
1 teaspoon of sweet marjoram,
3 teaspoons of chopped parsley,
Salt and cayenne pepper to the taste,
1 raw egg.

Split the plants and soak in salt and water 2

hours. Parboil them, peel and press all the water out. Chop them fine; mash the yolks of eggs and mix together. Add onion, parsley, and marjoram, rubbed and sifted. Add the raw egg, after beating well; then the melted butter, salt, and pepper. Put in baking-dish with grated cracker on top, and bake $\frac{1}{2}$ hour.

GREEN CORN CUSTARD
WITH BROILED TOMATOES
Mrs. Daniel B. Wentz

1 cupful of corn, freshly cut from the ears of
    young corn,
4 eggs, beaten slightly,
1 teaspoon of salt,
A little paprika,
A few drops of onion juice,
1¼ cups of milk.

Bake in buttered moulds in hot water. When firm, turn out and place on dish with broiled tomatoes around. Serve with cream sauce made as follows:

1 tablespoon of butter,
1 tablespoon of flour,
1 cup of milk.

Cook till thick.

HOMINY PUFFS

1 quart of cold boiled hominy,
4 heaping tablespoons of flour,
3 teaspoons of baking powder,
1 coffeecup of sweet milk,
1 teaspoon of salt,
4 eggs.

Take thoroughly cooked hominy when cold and stir in the well-beaten yolks, then flour, milk, and salt alternately with the baking-powder. Add last the whites of eggs beaten to a stiff froth and stirred in slowly. Have lard boiling and drop the mixture in with a spoon, and fry rich brown.

MACARONI

1 pound macaroni,
¼ pound butter,
¼ pound grated cheese.

Boil the macaroni till tender, and then put in a deep dish and spread over it pieces of butter and scatter the grated cheese. Put in another layer of macaroni, and so on. Put bits of butter on top, with salt and pepper, and bake well.

HOW TO COOK MACARONI

Mrs. Woodford Spears

Boil 14 short sticks or 24 long ones in salt water for 20 minutes. Drain off water and mix with

½ pint of grated cheese (light measure),
1 pint of cream (or 1 pint of new milk with ½ tablespoon of butter),
1 grated biscuit.

Place on top of stove and let it cook until it begins to thicken; then place in oven long enough to brown.

SPAGHETTI

For 4 persons, strain a can of tomatoes, add a suspicion of onion; stew 3 or 4 hours; add to the tomatoes a tablespoon of sugar and a little salt and a little butter. Boil macaroni 1½ hours; season with salt; pour tomatoes over it; grated Parmesan cheese on top. Serve tomato dressing without sugar for chops.

BROILED MUSHROOMS

Take fresh mushrooms, and after peeling them lay them in salted water for a few minutes. Wipe dry and season with salt and pepper, and dip in butter and broil over a hot fire. Serve with crisp toast.

STEWED MUSHROOMS

Peel fresh mushrooms. Put butter in saucepan and let it get hot. Put mushrooms in and stir till they become tender. Season with salt and pepper, and add 1 cup of cream and half a spoonful of flour. Let it simmer. Serve in a dish or on toast.

BOILED OKRA

Boil the okra in salt water for half an hour. Season with salt, pepper, and butter and serve hot.

OKRA AND CORN

E. D. P.

1 pint of sliced okra,
1 pint of cut corn,
½ cup of milk,
1 teaspoon of flour,
1 slice of pickled pork,
Salt and pepper to the taste.

Fry the pork and remove, leaving the grease in the pan. Fry the okra 10 minutes; then add corn and fry thoroughly. Mix the flour and milk and pour over okra and corn, and fry for 5 minutes. Season and serve.

A teacup of chopped fried tomatoes with the above, instead of the milk, is an improvement.

OKRA AND TOMATOES

Take equal parts of okra and tomatoes and cook separately. Peel the tomatoes and cut the okra in pieces first. Season with butter, salt, pepper, and a little onion, and place together in a dish and serve hot.

ONIONS FOR BREAKFAST

Take good-sized onions, peel and slice them and boil till tender. Put a layer of onions in a pan and cover with bread-crumbs, salt, pepper, and butter; then another layer of onions, and so on till pan is full. Pour over it a cup of cream and bake till brown.

STEWED ONIONS

Boil the onions in clear water. Change the water several times, and boil them till tender. Drain and season with butter, flour, salt and pepper, and cream. Let simmer till thick.

Serve hot with sauce poured over onions.

POTATO CHIPS

Take nice smooth potatoes, peel them, and slice very thin with a machine for the purpose, or a cabbage-cutter. Throw in cold water. Pour boiling water on them till they are clear. Then pour ice water on them to crisp them. Wipe dry and drop one at a time into boiling lard and cook a pretty brown.

POTATOES BAKED IN THEIR JACKETS

After washing and drying potatoes, put them in a pan and set in oven for an hour or more. Remove when the skins break easily. If greased with either lard or butter they will bake quickly. If mashed with the hands on taking from the oven they will be very mealy. Wrap in a napkin. Serve hot.

STEWED POTATOES

Pare, cut in dice, and soak in cold water $\frac{1}{2}$ hour; stew in enough hot salted water to cover them; before taking up, and when they are breaking to pieces, drain off the water, and pour in a cup of rich milk and butter the size of a hen's egg; boil 3 minutes, stirring well; roll the butter in flour, add a little salt and pepper, boil up well, and turn into a hot dish.

STUFFED POTATOES

Take large potatoes, bake until soft; cut a round piece off the top of each; scrape out the inside very carefully so as not to break the skin, and set aside the empty cases; mash the inside very smoothly, working into it while hot some butter and cream, about a teaspoon of each for every potato; season with salt and pepper, with a good pinch of cheese grated for each; work it very soft with cream and put into saucepan to heat, stirring hard to prevent burning; when scalding hot, stir in one well-beaten egg for six large potatoes; boil up once; fill the skins with the mixture and return them to the oven for 3 minutes; arrange in pretty napkin with caps uppermost; cover with fold of napkin; stand them up in something while heating.

POTATOES EN SURPRISE

Season 1 pint of hot mashed potatoes with 1 tablespoon of butter, 1 teaspoon of salt, $\frac{1}{4}$ teaspoon celery salt, $\frac{1}{4}$ teaspoon pepper, and very little cayenne, 6 drops onion juice; add yolk of one egg; shape into round balls like croquettes; fill centre with creamed chicken, peas, or sweetbreads; dip into crumbs, or eggs and crumbs, and fry in hot lard.

GREEN PEPPERS STUFFED WITH CORN

Mrs. Daniel B. Wentz

To 6 medium-sized peppers take 1 can of corn, or enough fresh corn to fill them. Boil the peppers with a little soda to soften them. Mix the corn; add pepper, salt, and butter to taste.

Fill the peppers. Fill a baking-dish half full of water; put the peppers in and bake.

Serve with a cream sauce.

146

DELICIOUS WAY TO COOK RICE

E. D. P.

½ cup of rice,
2 quarts of boiling water,
2 teaspoons of salt.

Wash the rice through two waters. Put the rice
in the boiling water gradually, so as not to stop the
boiling, and let it boil 20 minutes without stirring.
Then drain through colander, rinse with cold water,
and shake free from water. Put back in saucepan
and let it stand on back of stove for 5 minutes.

SALSIFY

Boil in hot water with a little salt. Scrape and
cut in rings. Stew in new milk and season with
butter, flour, salt, and pepper. Serve hot.

SALSIFY FRITTERS

Boil the salsify and then scrape it and mash into
a batter. Add 2 eggs, pepper, and salt, and thick-
en with 1 tablespoon of flour. Fry in hot lard.

SPINACH

Wash through several waters, and put in boiling water with a small piece of pork. Boil quickly, and when done season with butter, salt, and pepper, and serve with poached eggs.

CREAMED SPINACH

Put in boiling water and boil till tender. Drain and chop fine and season highly with butter, salt, and pepper. Serve on toast.

SUCCOTASH

Take $\frac{1}{2}$ gallon of beans, string them carefully, and break into short pieces. Add $\frac{1}{2}$ pound bacon and cover with water. Put in a kettle and boil for $2\frac{1}{2}$ hours, or till nearly dry, when add the corn cut from 6 cobs. Season with salt, pepper, 1 cup of cream, 1 tablespoon flour, and let it boil $\frac{1}{2}$ hour.

BAKED TOMATOES

Peel the tomatoes and make a hole in the centre of each and fill with bread-crumbs, salt, pepper, butter, and a little sugar. Put in dish and bake 2 hours.

A TYPICAL BLUE GRASS COOK

FRIED GREEN TOMATOES

Slice green tomatoes and lay them in salt water. Drain and sprinkle with sugar. Roll in corn meal and fry in hot lard. Salt and pepper to taste.

FRIED TOMATOES

Mrs. Henry C. Buckner

Cut fresh tomatoes in thick slices. Fry $\frac{1}{2}$ hour in little butter and take out of frying-pan. Stir into what is left in frying-pan 1 teaspoon of flour moistened in milk. Add a little milk. When consistency of cream sauce, pour over tomatoes.

SCALLOPED TOMATOES

Peel and slice the tomatoes. Grate bread-crumbs on them and season highly with sugar, butter, cayenne pepper, and salt. Alternate the layers of tomatoes and bread-crumbs and bake in a dish for 2 hours.

Salads

CAULIFLOWER SALAD

Cook the cauliflower in boiling water till tender. Drop in cold water. Pull it apart and dry with a cloth. Serve with mayonnaise or French dressing.

CELERY SALAD

Cut crisp celery into short lengths and put on ice. When ready to serve, mix through it either mayonnaise or French dressing made of 2 table-spoons olive oil and 1 of vinegar, and salt and pepper to taste.

CHICKEN SALAD (No. 1)

Take young chickens and boil till tender. Remove them, and when cool cut into 1 inch pieces.

To 1 pint of meat add $\frac{3}{4}$ pint of celery. Season highly with pepper and salt. Mix the celery and meat lightly and put on ice. Just before serving mix a good mayonnaise lightly through it. Serve on crisp lettuce leaves with a spoon of mayonnaise on each leaf.

CHICKEN SALAD (No. 2)

E. D. P.

1 well-boiled chicken,
2 teacupfuls of celery cut in dice,
2 teacupfuls of cream,
1 tablespoonful of mixed mustard,
2 heaping tablespoonfuls of butter,
Vinegar, salt, and cayenne pepper to the taste,
The yolks of 4 eggs.

Put the cream into a saucepan, and when it comes to a boil stir in the butter, vinegar, salt, and cayenne pepper, lastly the well-beaten eggs; stir well until it becomes like thick boiled custard; then take it off the fire; put the saucepan in cold water and stir until it cools, so as to keep it from curdling; take off the skin and fat of the chicken, cut it in dice, and with the celery mix carefully with the dressing.

COLD SLAW (No. 1)

Take off the outer leaves and split the head of a cabbage and cut on a slaw-cutter or with a sharp knife into fine shreds and put on ice. Serve with French dressing or mayonnaise.

COLD SLAW (No. 2)

Prepare as for any slaw, and pour over it a dressing made of

½ pint vinegar,
2 eggs beaten well with 1 teaspoon of made mustard,
½ teaspoon pepper,
1 teaspoon salt,
1 teaspoon sugar.

When the vinegar boils, add ingredients and cook till thick. Slice 5 hard-boiled eggs and put on top. Pour dressing over and serve at once.

EGG SALAD

Take any number of hard-boiled eggs and remove the shells and cut in halves. Remove carefully the yellows and make a dressing of them with chopped ham, pepper, and salt, made mustard, butter, and a little cream. Mix well and fill the whites. Put on ice till ready to serve. Serve on lettuce leaves with French dressing or mayonnaise.

FRUIT SALAD (No. 1)

Equal parts of fruit, Malaga grapes, celery, oranges, and nuts. Dressing of sugar, lemon juice, oil, and vinegar. Just before using, mix with whipped cream.

FRUIT SALAD (No. 2)

Mrs. James E. Clay

$1\frac{1}{2}$ pints cut celery,
$\frac{3}{4}$ pint cut pineapple,
$\frac{1}{2}$ pint shelled pecans.

Use mayonnaise or French dressing with sugar and red pepper in it.

FRUIT SALAD (No. 3)

Take equal parts of apples and celery and cut in small pieces. Serve on lettuce leaves with French dressing.

GRAPE-FRUIT AND ENGLISH WALNUT SALAD

Mrs. Henry C. Buckner

Take out the sections, being careful to remove all the white, bitter skins. To 1 quart of grape-fruit, after it is prepared, add 1 pint of English walnuts.

Serve with bleached lettuce and a French dressing made of lemon in the proportion of 3 tablespoons of oil to 1 of lemon juice.

LOBSTER SALAD

1 can of lobster,
Equal part of celery.

Chop the lobster and cut the celery. Serve on lettuce leaves with a rich mayonnaise.

NUT SALAD

Take equal parts of celery and nuts and serve on lettuce leaves with a French dressing.

155

ORANGE SALAD

Mrs. William E. Simms

Take fresh, firm oranges and peel them carefully down to the pulp, removing all the white skin. Hold the orange with a fork and with a sharp knife cut down on each side of the section and remove the pulp, taking care to keep its shape. Go over the whole orange this way. Serve on lettuce leaves with a dressing of olive oil and lemon, using 2 tablespoons of oil to 1 of juice. Add pecan nuts to the dressing.

POTATO SALAD (No. 1)

Mrs. George Dabney.

1 quart cold potatoes,
½ pint cold peas which have been cooked till tender,
2 or 3 good-sized, firm tomatoes, not too ripe,
2 stalks of celery,
1 onion chopped fine.

Cut the potatoes, tomatoes, and celery into small pieces, add the onion and season with salt and pepper. Serve on lettuce leaves with a rich mayonnaise.

POTATO SALAD (No. 2)

Take cold potatoes and cut into small pieces. Add chopped onion, salt, and pepper and put in a cool place. Before serving mix thoroughly with mayonnaise or French dressing.

Serve on lettuce leaves.

SALMON SALAD

1 can of salmon.

Remove the skin and bones and pick into small pieces.

Yolks of 6 hard-boiled eggs,
1 cup butter.

Mash eggs and butter and add salmon with pepper and salt and 1 tablespoon made mustard.

Serve on lettuce leaves.

SHRIMP SALAD

Mrs. Strauder Goff

Mix a pint of shrimps with a teacup of mayonnaise dressing. Arrange in the centre of a flat dish lined with lettuce leaves and put a row of peeled tomatoes around, showing the lettuce leaves around the edge of the dish. A few nasturtiums stuck in the centre add to the dainty look of the dish, and their colors harmonize with the red tomatoes and the pink shrimps. If the tomatoes are not uniform in size, they look better sliced.

TOMATO SALAD (No. 1)

Take 12 large ripe tomatoes. Remove skin and cut the centre from each. Fill the hole with a dressing of

1 cup cold ham, which has been run through a
    meat-grinder,
1 tablespoon chopped onion,
Salt and pepper to taste,
1 teaspoon celery seed,
½ cup of bread-crumbs,
1 tablespoon olive oil.

Put on ice and serve with a rich mayonnaise.

TOMATO SALAD (No. 2)

A good winter salad is made of

    1 can tomatoes,
    ½ box gelatine,
    1 tablespoon chopped onion,

1 teaspoon salt,
1 teaspoon white pepper.

Pour all into a granite kettle and heat well, almost to boiling point. Strain and pour into individual tin moulds. When congealed, serve on lettuce leaves with mayonnaise.

VEGETABLE SALAD

Line a bowl with lettuce leaves and put on them young onions, radishes, and cucumbers sliced thin. Serve with French dressing and crisp crackers.

Dressings for Salads

DRESSING FOR MEATS OR SALADS

Mix a heaping teaspoon of mustard, 1 of salt, and 1 of sugar together. Add a little red pepper and enough vinegar to make a paste. Beat yolks of 5 eggs and add mustard, etc., $\frac{1}{2}$ teacup of vinegar, 1 of rich cream, sour or sweet, and a piece of butter the size of an egg.

Boil till thick, and let it cool. It can be bottled and kept in cool place, and used as needed.

FRENCH DRESSING

4 tablespoons olive oil,
1 tablespoon of vinegar.

Season to taste with pepper, salt, and a little garlic. The bowl in which the dressing is to be made rubbed with garlic will give sufficient flavor.

MAYONNAISE

Mrs. Henry C. Buckner

Yolk of 1 egg,
½ teaspoonful of salt,
Dash of cayenne pepper,
1 cupful of salad oil,
½ teaspoonful of lemon juice

Let the oil and egg be very cold before using.
Also the plate must be on ice; let the yolk be entirely free from any white. Add salt and pepper
to egg and mix well, then add oil, drop by drop.
The success depends on adding the oil slowly at
first. Spend half of the time in incorporating the
first 2 spoonsful of oil; after that, it can be added
a little faster. After it is thick, alternate a few
drops of lemon juice or vinegar with the oil. A
little tarragon vinegar is nice. If mustard is liked
add ¼ teaspoonful of dry mustard with the salt at
the beginning. Some like a hard-boiled egg added
to the raw egg.

MRS. JACKSON'S SALAD DRESSING

1 teaspoon of dry mustard,
1 teaspoon of salt (scant measure),

162

1 tablespoon of sugar,

Beat with the yolks of 2 raw eggs,

Add a scant ½ cup of butter or oil, a few drops at a time,

The beaten whites of the eggs,

½ cup of vinegar, or lemon juice, beating well all the time.

Cook over boiling water until it thickens.

Ice Cream

ALMOND ICE CREAM

$\frac{1}{2}$ gallon of cream,
1 cup of grated almonds,
3 or 4 bitter almonds,
7 oranges.

Sweeten the cream and freeze. When nearly stiff enough, beat the almonds and juice in and freeze well.

APRICOT ICE CREAM

$\frac{1}{2}$ gallon of cream,
$\frac{1}{2}$ pint sugar,
1 can of apricots,
1 lemon,
1 tablespoon gelatine.

Make a syrup of the sugar and add the lemon juice. Mash and strain the apricots. When the syrup is cool, pour into the cream and put in the freezer. When half frozen, add the apricots and freeze quite hard.

BANANA ICE CREAM

A good banana cream is made by recipe for Apricot Cream. Use the lemon for flavoring. To ½ gallon of cream use 8 bananas. Mash the fruit, and add when the cream is half frozen.

BISCUIT GLACÉ (No. 1)

Mrs. Henry C. Buckner

1 quart of very rich cream,
Yolks of 6 eggs,
½ pound (scant) sugar, powdered,
2 tablespoons of vanilla,
2 dozen macaroons.

Beat eggs, sugar, and vanilla together until very light. Then whip the cream till very stiff, and add macaroons rolled very fine. Mix the eggs and sugar with the cream. Do not stir them in—or the cream will not remain stiff—but take a knife and turn the mixture in. Have ready a bucket; fill it, and pack immediately in ice and salt. Have the ice all ready before whipping the cream, as it must not stand. Use a quantity of salt, as it needs to freeze quite hard, and there is not the body to it there is to ice cream.

BISCUIT GLACÉ (No. 2)

Mrs. R. H. Hanson

1½ dozen stale macaroons,
½ pint of cream,
½ box Cox's gelatine.

Roll the macaroons very fine and add the cream and soak well. Dissolve the gelatine in water, then mix well with cream and almonds. Add ½ gallon cream which has been sweetened to taste, and freeze well.

BURNT ALMOND CREAM

Mrs. John T. Hedges

½ gallon of very rich cream,
6 tablespoons of granulated sugar,
¼ pound of blanched almonds.

Stir almonds and sugar over the fire until sugar is caramel-brown. Let it cool; pound in a mortar to a powder; add a little cream first, then the remainder already sweetened. Freeze.

167

If the cream is not rich, make a custard of

Yellows of 3 eggs,
$\frac{1}{2}$ cup of sugar,
1 quart of sweet milk.

Add to former when cool. Freeze.

CARAMEL ICE CREAM

1 quart cream,
1 quart morning's milk,
$\frac{1}{2}$ pint of brown sugar.

Boil the milk. Brown the sugar beat up into the boiling milk, and add 1 tablespoon gelatine. Add $\frac{1}{2}$ cup white sugar. Flavor with vanilla. When cool, strain into the cream and freeze.

FROZEN CUSTARD
WITH FRUIT

Make custard of

Yolks of 4 eggs,
1 quart of new milk,
$\frac{1}{2}$ pound of granulated sugar.

Boil the milk, add sugar, and stir in well-beaten eggs. Add to custard 1 tablespoon of gelatine in

a little cold milk, and let it cool. Put in freezer.
When half frozen add

> 1 cup of raisins,
> 1 cup of strawberry preserves,
> 1 cup of candied cherries,
> A little thinly sliced citron.

A little wine or sherry is an improvement. Stir
in last 1 pint of whipped cream. Freeze hard.

FROZEN PUDDING

Make a rich custard by any recipe and put in
freezer. When beginning to freeze add

> ½ cup raisins,
> 1 pound almonds, chopped fine,
> 1 quart whipped cream.

Stir well to prevent fruit from going to bottom.
Before the cream is too stiff, add seasoning of good
whisky. Put the whisky last, as it prevents
freezing.

FRUIT ICE CREAM

Mrs. John W. Fox

> ½ gallon of rich cream,
> 1 cup sugar,

$\frac{1}{2}$ teacup of whisky,

1 teacup of raisins or cherries.

Make a syrup of the sugar and add 1 tablespoon gelatine. Flavor with vanilla. When syrup is cool, pour into the cream. Put in the freezer, and when it is half frozen, add the fruit and half of the whisky.

After a few turns of the freezer, add the rest of the whisky. Whisky is hard to freeze, and must be put in as directed.

LEMON ICE CREAM

2 quarts milk,

4 eggs,

$\frac{3}{4}$ pound sugar.

Beat the eggs together. Boil the milk and add 1 tablespoon gelatine. Beat the eggs and sugar and add to the boiling milk. When cool, add the juice of 5 lemons and 1 orange. Put in the freezer, and when half frozen, add 1 pint whipped cream.

MACAROON ICE CREAM

E. D. P.

$\frac{1}{2}$ gallon of rich cream,

1 dozen waxy macaroons,

3 large oranges,
½ teaspoon of vanilla,
½ pound of sugar.

Put the sugar in the cream and whip it up in whip-churn, or beat with an egg-beater as you would for egg-nog. Freeze. Let orange juice, vanilla, and sugar soak with the crushed macaroons and add when cream is half frozen. Freeze smoothly and pack till ready to serve.

MAPLE MOUSSÉ

Mrs. Henry C. Buckner

Whip 1 pint of cream; drain it well. Beat the yolks of 4 eggs light. Put into a saucepan a generous cup of maple syrup; stir in the beaten yolks, and place over the fire. Stir until the mixture becomes hot and the eggs thicken the syrup. Take from the fire at once and stand the pan in ice water, and beat the mixture with an egg-beater until it is light and cold; then gently mix with it the whipped cream, and mould for 4 or 6 hours, packed well in ice and salt.

MARCELLUS'S CHOCOLATE ICE CREAM

1 gallon rich cream,
½ cake of chocolate,
1 pint white sugar.

Make a syrup of the sugar with a little water, and add the melted chocolate and 2 tablespoons gelatine. Be sure that the chocolate is thoroughly melted, or it will be lumpy. When cool, stir into the cream and freeze. Flavor with vanilla.

METROPOLITAN ICE CREAM

1½ gallons cream.

Take ½ gallon and color with chocolate and flavor with vanilla.

½ gallon of cream and color with cochineal and flavor with rose.

½ gallon and flavor with lemon. Freeze each separately and then stack in a mould and put on ice and freeze again. Or take any other combination preferred and pack and freeze.

MARCELLUS

MRS. BASHFORD'S TUTTI-FRUTTI ICE CREAM

Yolks of 6 eggs,
2 pints of fresh sweet milk,
Sugar to taste,
1 teacup of raisins,
1 pound of almonds (in the shell), blanched and
    powdered rather fine,
1 teacup of strawberry preserves.

Make a custard of the eggs, milk, and sugar, and pour hot on the raisins, almonds, and preserves. Flavor with vanilla. Let it cool and then freeze. When nearly frozen, have ready 3 pints of good rich cream, sweetened and whipped. Pour into custard and continue freezing, stirring often.

TUTTI-FRUTTI ICE CREAM

1 quart cream,
1 pint milk,
Yolks of 5 eggs,
3 cups sugar,
1 lemon,
1 glass whisky.

Crystallized fruit or candied fruit of any kind, cherries, raisins, currants, citrons, peaches, etc.

Beat sugar and eggs together and add to the milk, which must be at boiling point. Boil 10 minutes. When cold, add the cream and freeze. When half frozen, add 1 pound fruit, which has been mixed with the lemon and whisky. Cover and freeze well.

NESSELRODE PUDDING (No. 1)

Mrs. Richard Thornton

- 2 ounces raisins,
- 2 ounces currants,
- 2 ounces candied citron,
- 2 ounces ginger,
- 2 ounces pineapples,
- 2 ounces peaches,
- 2 ounces apricots,
- 2 ounces cherries,
- 2 ounces orange peel.

Pour over this 3 glasses Maraschino cordial and let it stand over night. Pulverize 4 dozen almonds, which have been blanched. Add $\frac{1}{2}$ pound sugar and a vanilla bean and sift.

Make a custard of 1 quart milk,
Yolks 12 eggs.

Boil the milk, heat the eggs and sugar, almonds

and bean, and stir all into the boiling milk. Boil
till it thickens, and strain and put in a freezer.
Whip 4 pints thick cream and stir in fruit and
add to the custard. Mash macaroons and stir in
at same time. Freeze all together.

This recipe can be simplified by adding only
raisins and one kind of candied fruit and flavor
with brandy.

NESSELRODE PUDDING (No. 2)

E. D. P.

1 quart of milk,
Yolks of 12 eggs,
½ pound of sugar,
48 Spanish chestnuts or equal in common chest-
    nuts,
3 glasses of Maraschino,
12 waxy meringues,
3 pints of whipped cream.

Make custard of milk, eggs, and sugar. Blanch
chestnuts like almonds and add to custard. When
half frozen, add meringues, Maraschino, and cream
and freeze hard.

NICE FOUNDATION
FOR ICE CREAM

1 pint of morning's milk,
½ pint of sugar,
Yolks of 2 eggs,
1 quart rich cream.

Make a custard and flavor with vanilla bean. When cold, add 1 quart of whipped cream. Add fruits, nuts, wine, or anything desired, and freeze well.

This amount will serve 8 people.

NUT ICE CREAM

Mrs. Henry C. Buckner

1 pint of cream,
½ cup of almonds,
¼ cup of gelatine,
6 tablespoons of Maraschino, **or**
4 tablespoons of sherry,
⅓ cup of granulated sugar,
1 teaspoon of vanilla.

Put cream on ice and whip. Soak gelatine in 1 pint of cold water 1 hour. Cover while soaking.

Add wine and vanilla to sugar. Add these to cream, then the nuts, chopped fine. Put red cherries on top.

ORANGE ICE CREAM

> 1 quart of morning's milk,
> 1 pint rich cream,
> Juice of 5 oranges,
> 1 lemon,
> 1 pound sugar.

Boil the milk and add 1 tablespoon gelatine. When cool, dissolve sugar in the milk. Add the orange juice with the grated rind of one orange and the juice and the rind of 1 lemon. Put in freezer, and when it begins to freeze add the cream, which has been well whipped, and continue freezing.

ORANGE SOUFFLÉ

Mrs. Henry C. Buckner

> Yolks of 4 eggs, well beaten,
> 1 pint (full) of orange juice,
> 1 pound of sugar,
> ½ box of gelatine,
> 1 quart of whipped cream.

Cover gelatine for 1 hour with ½ cup of cold

water. Mix orange juice and sugar, add eggs, then beat in gelatine and let cool in ice water. When it begins to thicken, beat in lightly the whipped cream and freeze.

MARCELLUS'S PEACH ICE CREAM

1 gallon very rich cream,
½ gallon ripe peaches and juice of a lemon,
1 pound or more of sugar, the amount depends on the sweetness of the fruit.

Make a syrup as in other recipes, and when cold add the cream and put in the freezer. Mash the peaches and add the lemon and a little sugar. When the cream is half frozen, add the fruit and freeze. Very good.

PINEAPPLE ICE CREAM

Mrs. John W. Fox

2 quarts rich cream,
4 cups sugar,
2 cans of pineapple or two ripe pineapples.

Make a syrup of the sugar and add 1 tablespoon gelatine. Add juice of 1 lemon and boil. When

178

cool, add half of the cream and put in the freezer. When it begins to freeze, add the pineapple, which has been chopped very fine, and after a few turns add the rest of the cream, which has been well whipped.

PISTACHIO ICE CREAM

Mrs. Henry C. Buckner

Make a custard of

> 1 pint of morning's milk,
> ½ pint of white sugar,
> Yolks of 2 eggs.

Pound ½ of a vanilla bean and boil with the custard. When cold, color a delicate green with pure fruit coloring. Add 1 quart of rich whipped cream. Put in freezer, and when it begins to congeal add
1 teacup of sweet almonds, and
1 teacup of pistachio nuts, blanched and powdered.
Freeze hard.

RASPBERRY ICE CREAM

Make as for any other kind of fruit cream and add the fruit when half frozen. Mash and strain the berries and add a little lemon juice.

STRAWBERRY ICE CREAM

> 1 quart strawberries,
> 1 quart cream,
> 1 pint sugar.

Cap the berries and sprinkle over them 1 cup of sugar and let stand 1 hour.

Mash and strain through cloth till pulp remaining is about the size of an egg. Make a syrup of the sugar, and when cool add the cream. Put in freezer, and when half frozen add the fruit and freeze hard.

SULTANA ROLL
OR FROZEN WATERMELON

Mrs. W. A. Johnson

Make a plain cream by scalding 1 pint of milk. Mix

> 1 tablespoon of flour,
> 1 cup of sugar,
> ¼ teaspoon of salt,
> 1 beaten egg.

Pour over this the scalded milk. In a double boiler cook until it thickens, stirring often. Cool and add 1 quart of cream. Flavor with 1 tablespoon of vanilla and 1 tablespoon of almond extract. Freeze.

Line a melon-mould that has been embedded in ice and salt with the frozen cream about an inch thick. Sprinkle over this raisins that have been soaked in brandy or wine 1 hour. Fill in the centre with whipped cream, which has been sweetened and flavored. Cover over the top with the frozen cream. Cover the mould with greased paper; fasten on top securely, and keep packed in ice and salt for 3 hours.

VANILLA CREAM

1½ pints of cream,
1 ounce of isinglass,
1 pound of sugar (or ¾ pound),
Yolks of 4 eggs,
½ pint of milk,
Flavor with vanilla.

Just scald the cream; dissolve all the isinglass in the milk, and pour it on the sugar and eggs beaten together to a froth. Add the flavoring. Strain, cool; add a quart of whipped cream, and freeze it; then pack it for 3½ hours at least.

ICE CREAM

Mrs. H. C. McDowell

Make custard of the yolks of 3 eggs,
1 pint of milk,
Flavor with vanilla and sweeten to taste.

Let the custard stand 1 hour and then add 3 pints of whipped cream. Pour into the freezer, and when nearly frozen add $\frac{1}{2}$ teacup of cherries, $\frac{3}{4}$ cup of almonds, $\frac{3}{4}$ cup of rum, or some rum and sherry mixed.

Almonds and cherries must be chopped fine.
Freeze stiff and serve.

Ices, Punches, and Sherbets

CHAMPAGNE ICE

Make a syrup of 1 pound sugar, 1 quart water, and add juice of 3 oranges and 1 lemon. Boil a few minutes and strain into the freezer. When it begins to thicken, flavor with a small bottle of champagne.

CRANBERRY PUNCH

Mrs. Henry C. Buckner

3 pints of cranberries,
6 lemons.

Make quite sweet.

Boil cranberries in ½ gallon of water till tender. Strain through a sieve to get all the pulp, holding back the skins. Add the lemon juice and make as sweet as you would sherbet. Put in freezer and freeze well. Then take 1 wineglassful of fine whisky, ½ wineglass of old Jamaica rum, and beat in thoroughly, and pack in freezer till ready to serve.

CRÊME DE MENTHE PUNCH

Mrs. Henry C. Buckner

Make a nice lemon sherbet or ice and freeze till firm. Add

½ pint of creme de mint,
½ wineglass of Jamaica rum,

And turn dasher rapidly a few times.

When ready to serve, decorate with creme de mint cherries.

FROZEN EGG-NOG

Mrs. Henry C. Buckner

Yolks of 12 eggs,
1 pound of sugar,
1 pint of brandy,
1 pint of Jamaica rum,
1 gallon of cream.

Beat the yolks very light and add the sugar, then the whipped cream. Freeze till firm, and then add the brandy and rum, and turn freezer rapidly a few times to mix well.

Ready to serve.

GRAPE ICE

Mrs. Simms

1 quart of juice from fresh grapes,
4 lemons, juice only,
1 tablespoon of gelatine, dissolved in water.

Sweeten to taste. Mix well and freeze.

MADEIRA ICE

1 quart Madeira wine,
1 pint water,
½ pound sugar,
Juice of 1 lemon.

Make a syrup of sugar and water and add lemon juice. When cool, strain and put in freezer. When it begins to thicken, add 1 quart Madeira wine and freeze hard.

ORANGE ICE

Miss Annie Lyle

6 oranges,
2 lemons,
1 quart of water,
1 pint sugar.

Squeeze the fruit, being careful to remove the seed. Boil the water and pour over the sugar. When dissolved, let the water stand on the fruit for ½ hour. Strain and mix with the juice and freeze. This will make 2 quarts.

RASPBERRY ICE

Take enough berries to make a quart of juice. Add juice of 3 lemons and 1 pound sugar. Pour over 1 quart boiling water and let it stand 1 hour, and then strain into freezer and freeze hard.

ROMAN PUNCH

Make a strong lemonade, about a quart, and put in freezer. When half frozen, add whites of 4 eggs, well beaten, and 1 glass of Jamaica rum, juice of 3 oranges, and a small glass of champagne, if preferred, and freeze hard.

SHERBET

Miss Mary Bashford

1 quart of water
3 lemons,
2 teacups of sugar,
3 eggs.

Cook sugar to a candy. Stir it into whites of eggs as for icing. Season and freeze.

SHERRY PUNCH

Mrs. Campbell Carrington Cochran

1 quart of water and 2 cups of sugar boiled together 5 minutes. Remove from the fire and add

Juice of 6 oranges,
Juice of 3 lemons,
1½ pints of sherry.

Freeze.

STRAWBERRY ICE

Mash the berries and have 1 quart juice. Add juice of 2 lemons, 1 pound sugar. Pour over 1 quart boiling water and let it stand an hour. Strain and pour in freezer and freeze quite hard.

187

Creams and Other Desserts

BAVARIAN CREAM
WITH ALMONDS

Blanch 3 ounces of sweet and 1 ounce of bitter almonds, and skin them. Put them in a pan on a moderate fire, stirring constantly. As soon as they have acquired a fine yellow color, take off and let get cold. Pound them into fine pieces. Then add

1 pint of cream, nearly boiling,

2 or 3 tablespoons of sugar,

½ package of gelatine, previously washed in ½ cup of cold water.

Put upon the ice, and when ready to thicken stir till smooth. Have ready 1 pint of cream; whip and then stir it in; put into a mould and surround with ice.

BAVARIAN CREAM
WITH PINEAPPLE

Cut a pineapple into fine pieces. Boil it with ½ pound or coffeecup of sugar. Pass this marmalade through a sieve or colander. Turn off part of the juice and add ½ package of gelatine, dissolved in ½ cup of cold water. Stir, and add ½ pint of whipped cream as before described.

BEAUTIFUL CREAM

Make a foundation of pastry and a wall of cherries, oranges, and grapes. Fill with chestnuts, whipped cream, or a very rich ice cream.

BIVEAU CREAM

Boil

1 pint of water,
1 ounce of gelatine,
¼ of a vanilla bean,
½ pound of sugar.

When the mixture is almost cold, stir in 3 pints of thick cream, whipped to a stiff froth.

190

CHARLOTTE POLONAISE

Mrs. Henry C. Buckner

Yolks of 6 eggs,
2 large spoonfuls of cornstarch,
1½ pints of cream.

Beat the yolks till light; add the cornstarch and cream and boil slowly till it is thick and perfectly smooth, stirring all the time to prevent it becoming lumpy.

Divide the mixture in 2 parts. Make a chocolate filling of

4 to 6 ounces of chocolate,
Sweeten to taste,
¼ pound of macaroons.

Add to mixture and let it boil up, and set aside to cool.

With the other half make an almond filling of

1 dozen bitter almonds,
¼ pound of sweet almonds,
¼ pound of citron,
¼ pound of sugar.

Blanch and pound the almonds to a paste with the citron. Stir in the sugar and rest of mixture and let it come to a boil, and set aside to cool.

Make 6 layers of pretty white cake by any good

recipe. When baked cut the centres out, making a good-sized hole in each for the filling. Spread one layer thickly with the chocolate mixture, another with the almond filling, and stack them, being careful to put the mixture very thick on top. Cover the whole with a thick meringue and set in oven to harden. Remove from oven and let it cool.

Make a filling of 1 quart of whipped cream, highly seasoned with vanilla and a little wine, sugar, and any of the almond mixture that is left over. Fill the hole and let the cream come above the cake. The remainder can be served with the polonaise.

CHARLOTTE RUSSE

E. D. P.

2 yolks of eggs,
1 pint of new milk,
A small piece of vanilla bean,
¼ pound of sugar,
⅔ box of Cox's gelatine,
1 quart of rich cream.

Make a custard of the eggs, milk, and sugar. Dissolve the gelatine in a full half-pint of boiling water and strain into the custard. Beat the cream to a stiff froth; then stir into the custard when it is about blood heat. Line a bowl with lady fingers, pour in the mixture, and set away to cool. This is a winter dish and difficult to make in summer.

CHOCOLATE
BAVARIAN CREAM

Cover ½ box of gelatine with ½ teacup of water and let it soak 20 minutes. Whip 1 pint of cream. Grate 2 ounces of chocolate and boil in 1 pint of sweet milk. Add the gelatine and stir till dissolved. Take from the fire and sweeten with ½ cup of sugar; flavor with vanilla and turn into a pan to cool. Stir till it begins to thicken, then add the whipped cream. Stir till mixed, and pour in a bowl to harden.

Serve with whipped cream.

CHOCOLATE BLANC-MANGE
V. C. G.

Soak ½ box of Cox's gelatine,
1 quart of sweet milk,
½ cake of sweet chocolate,
½ cup of sugar.

Flavor to taste; mix milk, sugar, and chocolate, and let it boil nearly an hour. Strain through a sieve, pressing the sediment through with a spoon. Add the gelatine and vanilla when taking it off the stove. When nearly cold, put in a mould which has been wet with cold water.

MRS. BRUTUS CLAY'S CHARLOTTE RUSSE

Dissolve 1 ounce of gelatine in 1 pint of milk by boiling. Beat the yolks of 4 eggs (sweetened) and stir them in while the milk is on the fire. When this is cooked to the consistency of custard, strain into a bowl, stirring constantly. Season $\frac{1}{2}$ gallon of cream with whisky. Whip to a stiff froth and beat it in just as the custard (which should be seasoned with vanilla or rose water) begins to congeal. Have ready a glass bowl lined with sponge cake and pour in.

NICE WAY TO COOK APPLES

Mrs. James E. Clay

Put on 1 pint sugar to cook to a thick syrup. Add 6 or 8 nicely peeled pippin apples. Cover and cook till done and clear. Lift carefully, then add a few pieces of stick cinnamon and cook down thick and pour over apples. A few blanched almonds make a pretty dish. Serve with plain or whipped cream.

SPANISH CREAM

½ box of gelatine,
1 quart of milk,
Yolks of 3 eggs,
1 cup of sugar.

Soak the gelatine in the milk for an hour. Put on the stove and stir as it warms. Beat the yolks and sugar together and stir into the boiling milk. Flavor with vanilla. Pour into mould and serve with cream.

TAPIOCA AND APPLES

Soak ½ cup of tapioca in 1 quart of cold water over night. Add

4 or 5 apples cut in pieces.

Bake very slowly 2 hours. Let stand on ice 2 or 3 hours before using.

Serve with rich cream, either whipped or plain, as you may prefer.

195

VELVET CREAM

E. D. P.

1 cup of wine,
½ box of gelatine,
1 lemon,
1½ pints of milk,
1 cup of sugar.

Dissolve gelatine in the wine over the fire. Add peel and juice of lemon, and when gelatine has dissolved, add sugar. Let it simmer, then strain. Add the milk and stir till cold. Mould and let congeal. Serve with whipped cream.

Jellies

BEST WINE JELLY

E. D. P.

2   boxes of Cox's gelatine,
5   pints of water,
1   quart of sherry,
1   teacup of good whisky,
2   sticks of cinnamon,
4   cloves,
6   raisins,
Juice of 4 lemons,
1½ pounds of granulated sugar,
3   eggs.

Beat the whites of the eggs to a stiff froth and boil all together till the whites break away, and the jelly looks clear. Be careful not to let the gelatine stick to the bottom of the kettle. Stir constantly till it begins to boil. Pour in ½ cup of cold water and let it stand 5 minutes, then run through a jelly bag. Set on ice. Serve with whipped cream.

FRUIT JELLY

½ box gelatine,
1 lemon,
1 pint wine,
2 cups sugar,
2 pints water.

Boil gelatine, lemon and sugar. Flavor when taking from the stove, and when it begins to congeal stir in ½ pound white grapes.

MRS. PRESTON'S
WINE JELLY

1 pint of water,
½ pint of wine,
½ pint of whisky,
¼ pint of sugar,
3 lemons,
¾ box of Cox's gelatine,
Cinnamon to taste,
Whites of 3 eggs.

Boil, strain and set on ice. Serve with whipped cream.

CHURNING AT MOUNT AIRY, PARIS, KY.

NUT JELLY

1 box gelatine,
3 pints boiling water,
2 cups sugar,
Juice of 3 lemons.

Let it boil and then strain. Flavor with almond. When it begins to thicken, scatter nuts—English walnuts or cream nuts—through it and serve with whipped cream.

ORANGE JELLY

½ box of gelatine,
1 large cup of orange juice,
1 orange sliced thin,
1 lemon,
2 cups sugar,
1 pint hot water.

Put all in a kettle and let it come to a boil, and then strain and pour in mould to cool. Be sure to remove the seeds, as they are very bitter.

Serve with whipped cream and cocoanut cake.

WINE JELLY

Mrs. Ellet Cabell

Soak ½ box of gelatine in ½ cup of water. Add
½ pound of sugar and 2½ cups of boiling water.
Stir until gelatine is dissolved. Then add juice
of 1 lemon, 1 orange, ½ cup of sherry, 1 tablespoon brandy, 1 tablespoon of Maraschino. Add
last the beaten whites and crushed shells of 2 eggs.
When it has boiled a few minutes, remove from
the stove and strain into a mould and set on ice.
Serve with whipped cream.

Pastry

BAKED APPLE DUMPLINGS

Select firm acid apples and pare and core them and fill the holes with sugar, butter and cinnamon.

Take nice crust and roll into short pieces. Roll one about each apple and place in a deep pan and add enough warm water to cover. Sweeten the water to taste and add a small piece of butter. Bake in the oven till a light brown. Add more water if necessary. Serve with cold sauce made of

1 cup of sugar,
½ cup of butter.

Beat well together and flavor with lemon. A hot sauce may be used if preferred.

BLUE GRASS PASTRY

E. D. P.

1 pound of best flour,
¾ pound of butter,

1 wineglass of ice water,
Whites of 2 eggs.

Take ¾ pound of flour and put in a bowl. Put the other ¼ in a plate. Beat the eggs very light and mix in the flour with the water so as to make stiff dough. Beat well with a rolling-pin for 10 minutes. Roll, adding the butter in four rollings and the ¼ pound of flour. Set the pastry on ice for 2 hours.

This makes 3 pies.

PUFF PASTE

E. D. P.

1   pound of butter,
1½ pounds of flour,
½   pint of ice water.

Wash the butter carefully and squeeze out all the water. Divide in 6 parts. Separate the flour, leaving ½ pound to sprinkle with.

Take the 1 pound of flour and 1 piece of butter and mix with the ice water, using a knife for the purpose, and handle as little as possible.

Roll the paste from you and spread with the butter. Add ½ pound of flour in 3 rollings. Set in cool place for 1 or 2 hours.

When making pies, cut off only enough for one pie at a time, so as not to roll more than once after taking off the ice.

CHOCOLATE PIE (No. 1)

Mrs. James E. Clay

4 eggs,
2 cups of sugar,
½ cup butter,
1 cup of grated chocolate,
1 cup of cream.

Flavor with vanilla. Mix and cook in saucepan till it begins to thicken. Cook crust slightly, fill with the mixture and cook in oven till stiff. Cover with meringue.

CHOCOLATE PIE (No. 2)

Mrs. Strauder Goff

Stir the yolks of two well-beaten eggs, ⅓ of a cake of chocolate and a teacup of sugar into nearly a pint of new milk. Set over the fire and stir till it comes to a boil, then add 2 tablespoons of cornstarch dissolved in milk and ½ cup of butter. Let it cook till it thickens, stirring all the time. Then pour over the beaten whites of the eggs, set back on the stove for a few minutes, till the whites are cooked, and add a teaspoon of vanilla after taking off.

The pies made with this filling should be made with a top crust and are better served cold with cream, either plain or whipped. It makes a particularly attractive dessert made in little individual pie pans and served with frozen whipped cream.

COCOANUT PIE

E. D. P.

¼ pound of butter,

¼ pound of sugar, creamed with butter,

3 eggs, beaten well,

1 cup of rich milk, in which cocoanut has been soaked,

1 cocoanut grated.

Cook before putting in pastry.

CRANBERRY PIE

Miss Mary Bashford

1 teacup of sugar,

1 teacup of cranberries, or cherries,

½ teacup of raisins,

1 tablespoon of butter,
1 tablespoon of flour.

Cream butter, add flour, then sugar and cranberries. Put mixture in raw crust and bake with top. Cook 30 minutes in slow oven.

CREAM PIE (No. 1)

V. C. G.

1 quart of sweet milk,
2 eggs,
2 tablespoons of flour.

Mix the flour with some of the milk and let the remainder come to a boil. Beat the eggs light; put in the flour, and pour the boiling milk on these. Sweeten to taste and strain. Cook till thick as custard, stirring all the time. When cold, flavor with essence of lemon.

Bake a crust made of rich puff paste, and when cold, fill with the custard. The success of this depends on the cooking, and many good cooks slip a sharp knife under the crust here and there while it is cooking to make it light as possible.

CREAM PIE (No. 2)

Miss Mary Bashford

4 eggs—yolks only, leaving whites for a meringue,
1 pint of cream instead of butter,
3 kitchen spoons of flour,
¾ pint of sugar.
  Flavor and bake. Meringue on top.
  Make lemon pies the same way, using juice of
2 lemons.

IRISH POTATO PIE

1 pint mashed potatoes,
½ pint cream,
4 eggs,
¾ pound sugar,
1 orange,
1 cup of butter.

Cook and mash the potatoes. Beat the eggs together, add sugar and butter and beat well. Then pour in the cream and add the potatoes and stir well. Flavor with the juice of 1 orange. Bake in paste and cover with meringue of well-beaten whites of 2 eggs and 2 tablespoons sugar.

LEMON PIE (No. 1)

Mrs. R. H. Hanson

1   cup of buttermilk,
1½ cups sugar,
4   eggs,
1   tablespoon butter,
1   tablespoon cornstarch,
Juice and rind of 2 lemons.

Beat the yolks and reserve the whites for the meringue.

Add the other ingredients and cook in a porcelain pan till thick.

Fill the shells, spread the meringue on top and brown in the oven.

LEMON PIE (No. 2)

Miss Mary Bashford

6 eggs, using 2 whites,
2 lemons, if juicy—more, if dry,
1 pint of sugar,
½ pint of butter,
1 spoon of sifted flour.

Add lemon juice last. Cook and add meringue.

207

MINCE MEAT FOR PIES (No. 1)

R. V. J.

4 pounds of fresh tongue,
3 pounds of suet,
8 pounds of chopped apples,
3 pounds of currants,
4 pounds of seeded raisins,
6 pounds of white sugar,
2 pounds of citron, cut in small pieces,
4 lemons, grated rind and juice,
1 ounce of cinnamon,
$\frac{1}{4}$ ounce of cloves,
$\frac{1}{4}$ ounce of allspice,
4 nutmegs, grated,
1 quart of Madeira wine,
1 pint of cider,
1 quart of brandy or good whisky.

Boil the tongue in salted water until tender, and when cold, chop fine. Remove every particle of membrane from the suet and chop it fine, and mix with the tongue with enough salt to remove the fresh taste.

To this, add the apples, sugar, fruit, spices and other ingredients. Mix all together and cover close.

208

If too dry when ready for use, moisten with a little sweet cider.

MINCE MEAT FOR PIES (No. 2)

Mrs. Henry C. Buckner

5 pounds of beef tongue, cooked and chopped fine,
4 pounds of suet (be careful to remove strings),
2 pounds of raisins,
2 pounds of cherry preserves,
1 pound of damson preserves,
1 pound of peach preserves,
1 pound of pear preserves,
1½ pounds of ginger preserves,
1½ pounds of dried peaches, stewed,
1 pound of citron,
1 pound of currants,
2 nutmegs,
1 tablespoon of cinnamon,
1 tablespoon of cloves and spices, mixed,
5 pounds of white sugar.

Mix thoroughly with 1 pint of sherry wine and 1 pint of good whisky, and put in glass jars.

NUTMEG PIE

Mrs. Strauder Goff

3 eggs beaten separately,
1 pint sugar,
1 medium-sized nutmeg,
Piece of butter the size of an egg.

Mix, adding the whites last. This will make 2 pies.

ORANGE PIE

4 oranges,
1 quart milk,
2 tablespoons cornstarch,
3 eggs,
1 cup of sugar.

Peel, seed, and cut into small pieces the four oranges. Add the sugar and let it stand. Boil the quart of milk and stir in the cornstarch, which has been mixed with a little water. Add the yolks of the three eggs, which have been well beaten. Cook till a thick custard, and after cooled add the orange and sugar. Cook in pastry, and then make a meringue of the three whites and spread on top and brown slightly.

PUMPKIN PIE

Cut the pumpkin in small pieces and stew in a little water. Strain, and to 1 quart of the pumpkin add ½ pint of sugar, 1 cup of cream, cinnamon, and allspice to taste, 3 eggs, and 3 tablespoons butter. Beat it well. Line a pie-plate and pour the custard over it. Make a top with strips of pastry and bake till a rich brown.

STRAWBERRY SHORTCAKE

E. D. P.

Rub 2 tablespoons of butter in
    1 quart of flour, with
    ½ teaspoon of salt, and
    2 teaspoons of baking powder,
    Sweet milk enough for soft dough.

Mix lightly and put in pan the shape of Sally Lunn. Bake quickly. When done, split and butter while hot. In splitting any kind of hot bread, cut around the crust with a sharp knife and open carefully with a fork. Have fresh strawberries that have been well sweetened and spread over one-half; then lay on other half and spread with berries. Serve with whipped cream.

SWEET POTATO PIE (No. 1)
Mrs. J. W. Fox

For 2 pies take 4 large potatoes. Peel and steam them till mealy. Mash and beat or run them through a fruit-masher, and add

> 2 tablespoons butter,
> ½ cup of rich cream,
> ¼ cup white sugar,
> 2 eggs.

Season with cinnamon, spice, and nutmeg. Mix well and bake in a rich pastry. Cover top with a meringue of whites of 2 eggs beaten very stiff and sweetened with 2 tablespoons sugar.

SWEET POTATO PIE (No. 2)
(Famous Virginia Recipe)
Mrs. T. L. Rosser

> 1 pound boiled sweet potato,
> ¾ pound sugar,
> ¾ pound butter,
> 6 eggs,
> 1 lemon,
> 1 glass of brandy.

Rub the potatoes while hot through a colander. Cream the butter and sugar till very light and add to the potatoes. Beat 6 eggs till foamy and add to the mixture. Flavor with grated nutmeg, the juice and grated rind of 1 lemon, and add 1 glass of brandy.

Line a pie-plate with rich pastry and pour the ingredients in and bake in a moderate oven. When done, sprinkle the top with sugar and cover with fine bits of citron.

TRANSPARENT PIE (No. 1)

Mrs. Joseph Holt

Yolks of 8 eggs,
½ pound of butter,
1 pound of sugar,
1 wineglass of wine, flavored with lemon.
Mix well and cook in rich pastry.

TRANSPARENT PIE (No. 2)

E. D. P.

4 eggs, beaten separately,
1 cup of butter,
2 cups of sugar,
2 tablespoons of jelly.

Beat sugar and butter, then yolks, and add jelly. Bake in rich crusts with whites as a meringue.

WHIPPED CREAM PIE

Make a moderately rich pastry and cook and set aside to cool. Take 1 cup of rich sweet cream, which has been on ice for 1 hour, sweeten to taste, and flavor with vanilla and whip to a froth. Spread on the pie-crusts and serve. A little jelly placed in tiny bits over the pie adds to its appearance. This makes 2 pies.

WOODBURN
ORANGE SHORTCAKE

Mrs. Alexander J. Alexander

Make rich pie-crust and bake. Cut the oranges in sections, being careful to remove the white skins. Drain off the juice. Make a layer of the crust and then a layer of oranges, then crust and oranges. Cover top with icing, as for cakes. Serve hot or cold.

Make a syrup of the orange juice, sweeten to taste, and pour hot over the cake.

Do not stack the cake till just before serving, as the orange will soften the crust.

Puddings

ALMOND MANDALINES

Mrs. Henry C. Buckner

1½ cups of powdered sugar,
½ cup of butter,
¾ cup of milk,
4 eggs, or 8 yolks,
½ cup of cornstarch,
1½ cups of flour,
2 teaspoons of baking-powder,
1 teaspoon of vanilla.

Bake in 12 mandaline tins. When cold, cut off top with shell spoon, scrape out inside, fill with the following:

1 pint of whipped cream,
½ pound of almonds, grated,
½ cup of sugar,
½ teaspoon of vanilla.

Cover with top; frost with white icing.

215

A RICH AND DELICIOUS NUT PUDDING

Mrs. Henry C. Buckner

Beat separately 6 eggs; to the yolks add 1½ cups of granulated sugar. When the whites are very stiff, add 3 cups of finely chopped nuts. Mix all together lightly and stir in 1 teaspoon of vanilla. Last, stir in 1 teaspoon of baking-powder, well-mixed in 1 tablespoon of flour.

This is to be baked quickly in jelly-cake pans. It makes 3 layers. Put together with whipped cream. It takes a quart of cream. Season it with a little wine or whisky.

APPLE PUDDING

Mrs. W. T. Buckner

3 teacups of apples,
2 teacups of sugar,
1 teacup of butter,
7 eggs, leaving out 4 whites for meringue.

Cook in rich pastry and put meringue on top and brown.

BEATEN BISCUIT MACHINE, CUTTING
OUT THE BISCUIT

BLACK PUDDING

Mrs. James E. Clay

4 yolks of eggs,
1 teacup of sugar,
2 teacups of flour,
1 teacup of butter,
½ teacup of sour cream,
1 teacup of blackberry jam,
½ teaspoon soda,
Cinnamon, allspice, and cloves to taste.

Bake in pudding-pan or steam. Eat with white sauce seasoned with whisky.

BLUE GRASS PUDDING

E. D. P.

1 coffeecup of molasses,
1 coffeecup of sour cream,
1 full teaspoon of soda,
1 coffeecup of beef suet,
4 cups of flour,
1 pound of raisins,
¼ pound of citron,
1 pound of apples, chopped fine,

½ nutmeg,

2 teaspoons of cinnamon, or spices to taste.

Mix molasses, cream, and soda and let it foam. Add suet, flour, raisins, citron—having dredged them with flour—apples, and spices.

Grease mould well and let it steam 3 hours. Leave room for swelling. This quantity makes 2 puddings. Serve with sauce.

CABINET PUDDING

E. D. P.

½ pound of butter,

½ pound of sugar,

5 eggs,

½ cup of milk,

½ pound of sifted flour,

½ pound of raisins, seeded and dredged in flour.

Cream the butter and add sugar. Add well-beaten yolks, then milk, and by degrees the flour, alternately with the whites. Add the raisins and pour into well-buttered pudding-mould and boil 2½ hours. The mould should have a top. Put in kettle of boiling water. Keep the water within 1 or 2 inches of the top. The steam helps to cook the pudding, and the pot should be kept covered.

CARAMEL PUDDING

Mrs. Henry C. Buckner

1 full pint of rich milk or cream,
Yolks of 2 eggs,
2 tablespoons sugar,
1 tablespoon cornstarch,
Wine, macaroons, or any kind of preserved fruit.

Heat the milk in a double boiler. Beat the yolks very light and add the sugar. Stir the cornstarch with a little cold milk and add to the boiling milk, and add macaroons or fruit. Cook till thick. Make a meringue of the 2 whites and 4 tablespoons of sugar, cover the top and set in oven and brown slightly.

CHOCOLATE CUSTARD

V. C. G.

1 quart of milk,
4 eggs,
1½ bars of chocolate,
Sugar to taste.

Scald the milk and stir the chocolate in after it is grated. Beat the eggs and sugar together and stir into the milk, and let it cook till it is thick as boiled custard. Flavor with vanilla and pour into cups.

Serve cold with whipped cream.

CHOCOLATE ECLAIRS

Mrs. Walter E. Addison

Make sponge cake and flavor with lemon,
Make a filling of 1 quart of new milk,
Yolks of 4 eggs.

Boil the milk and add the yolks with 4 tablespoons sugar. When the milk has boiled, pour it on the yolks, stirring rapidly all the time. After well mixed return to the fire. Make a paste of 3 spoons cornstarch and cold milk and stir into the custard. Cook till well thickened. Flavor with vanilla.

Put a layer of this custard between the layers of cake. Cover the top with an icing made of 3 tablespoons chocolate, 6 of sugar, 2 of sweet cream, and a little butter.

CHOCOLATE PUDDING

E. D. P.

12 tablespoons of grated bread-crumbs,
6 tablespoons of grated vanilla chocolate,

1 cooking-spoon of butter,
1 quart of sweet milk,
Yolks of 6 eggs.

Boil the milk and sweeten to the taste with granulated sugar; then add the butter to it while boiling. Cool and add the well-beaten yolks of eggs and grated chocolate. Bake for ½ hour.

Beat the whites to a stiff froth, adding, while beating, 2 tablespoons of pulverized sugar. Spread over the pudding and brown nicely. Eat with cream.

STEAMED
CHOCOLATE PUDDING

Mrs. James E. Clay

Boil 1 quart of morning's milk and pour over 1
    pint sifted bread-crumbs,
¼ pound grated chocolate,
1 cup of sugar,
1 cup of flour,
1 cup of butter,
2 teaspoons baking-powder,
1 cup of raisins cut and seeded,
1 cup of pecans, and
2 tablespoons vanilla.

Steam 2 hours and serve with a rich sauce. Nuts

can be left out if desired. Pudding can be made several days before and steamed again when needed.

COCOANUT PUDDING

¼ pound of cocoanut, grated,
¼ pound of sugar,
3½ ounces of butter,
Whites of 6 eggs,
½ glass of wine and brandy, mixed.

Stir the butter and sugar to a cream. Stir the whites gradually. Then sprinkle cocoanut, stirring hard all the time. Serve with sauce.

COTTAGE PUDDING

Mrs. Joseph H. Holt

3 eggs (3 whites, 2 yolks),
1 quart of flour,
1 pint of sugar,
½ pint of butter (heaping),
1 cup of new milk,
1 teaspoon of cream of tartar,
½ teaspoon of soda.

Beat whites of eggs to stiff froth. Season all

with fresh lemon or whisky. Bake in buttered gem moulds and serve with rich sauce for cottage pudding.

DELICIOUS CREAM PUDDING

Mrs. James E. Clay

5 eggs,
1 tablespoon butter,
1 large cup of cream,
1 full pint of sugar,
2 tablespoons flour,
Season lightly with lemon.

Beat the yolks, saving the whites and half the sugar for the meringue. Add butter and sugar, then sift in flour, then lemon and cream. Pour in pudding-pan and bake. Add the meringue and brown slightly.

DIXIE PUDDING

1 pint bread-crumbs,
1 quart milk,
1 tablespoon sugar,
Yolks of 6 eggs.

Stir the bread-crumbs into the boiling milk, add the sugar and well-beaten yolks. Flavor with

223

vanilla and bake till it begins to thicken. Add 2 cups of sugar to the 6 whites which have been well beaten. Cover the top of pudding with acid jelly and spread on the meringue and stick almonds here and there on the top. Let it brown and serve cold with cream or sauce. A little wine may be used by leaving out the same quantity of milk.

FIG PUDDING

3 eggs,
1 scant coffeecup of sugar,
1 cup of sweet milk,
1 cup of butter,
2 heaping cups of bread-crumbs,
1 pound of figs, chopped fine,
1 wineglass of sherry,
2 tablespoons of flour, with
2 teaspoons of baking-powder, sifted in the flour.

Steam 3 hours. Serve with sauce.

Put pudding in a cake-mould and set in steamer.

FINE
ENGLISH PLUM PUDDING
V. C. G.

½ pound of flour,
¾ pound of bread-crumbs,

KNEADING BEATEN BISCUIT

6 ounces of suet, chopped fine,
1 pound of seeded raisins,
½ pound of currants,
¼ pound of citron, chopped fine,
¼ teaspoon of nutmeg,
½ teaspoon of cinnamon,
½ teaspoon of salt,
½ glass of brandy,
½ cup of light brown sugar,
3 eggs, well beaten,
1 pint of sweet milk,
Grated rind of 1 orange or lemon.

Steam constantly 4 or 5 hours. Eat with brandy sauce.

This is a splendid recipe.

FLOAT

V. C. G.

3 eggs,
1½ pints of milk,
1 cup of sugar,
Heaping tablespoon of cornstarch.

Flavor with vanilla. Cook till thick. Serve in glasses.

INDIAN PUDDING

R. V. J.

Boil 1 cup of meal in 1 pint of milk till it thickens. Add ½ cup of sugar, ½ cup of molasses, 1 tablespoon of butter, 1 pint of cold milk, salt to taste.

Steam and serve with hard sauce.

JEFF DAVIS PUDDING

3 eggs,
2½ teacups of sugar,
1 teacup of cream,
1 small cup of butter,
3 tablespoons of flour.

Season with lemon or nutmeg.

KENILWORTH PUDDING

E. D. P.

1 cup of apples, chopped fine,
1 cup of sweet milk,
1 cup of sugar,
1 cup of bread-crumbs,
1 cup of raisins or currants,

2 eggs, well beaten,
Butter size of an egg,
1 teaspoon of cinnamon.

Bake ½ hour. Serve hot with wine sauce.

LADY LEE PUDDING

R. V. J.

1   cup of suet, chopped fine,
1   cup of molasses,
1   cup of milk, with teaspoon of soda,
1   cup of raisins, currants, and citron, mixed,
2½ cups of flour.

Boil 3 hours.

NUT PUDDING

6   eggs,
1½ cups of sugar,
3   cups grated almonds or pecans,
Teaspoonful vanilla,
Teaspoonful baking-powder,
1   tablespoon flour.

Beat the yolks and add the sugar. Beat the whites very stiff and add the nuts. Mix all lightly and add baking-powder and flour. Bake in layers and fill with heavy whipped cream seasoned with whisky or brandy and pile around the cake. Sweeten the cream.

ORANGE PUDDING

R. V. J.

4 sweet oranges, sliced,
1 quart of milk,
1 cup of sugar,
2 tablespoons of cornstarch,
Yolks of 3 eggs.

Heat the milk; when nearly boiling add cornstarch (wet with a little cold water), the sugar, and eggs well beaten. Boil till thick as custard, and when cold pour over sliced oranges.

Make a meringue of the whites of 3 eggs and small teacup of sugar. Spread on pudding and decorate with sections of orange.

PLUM PUDDING

Mrs. Strauder Goff

1 pound raisins,
1 pound sugar,

228

1 pound suet,
1 pound currants,
½ pound citron,
½ pound bread-crumbs or flour,
6 eggs,
½ nutmeg,
2 teaspoons mixed spices,
1 tumbler of wine and whisky, mixed.

Steam 4 hours and serve with hard sauce. 2 teaspoons of baking-powder is an addition if the pudding is to be used soon after making. These puddings may be made in moulds or bags of the required size and kept in a cool place. Heat thoroughly when used.

PRUNE PUDDING (No. 1)

Mrs. James E. Clay

Whites of 5 eggs, beaten very stiff.

Add ½ pint granulated sugar and beat well. Stir in ½ teaspoon vanilla; lastly, add 1 dozen prunes, after being cooked and strained. Put in a baking-dish and set in a pan of warm water and cook 20 or 30 minutes.

PRUNE PUDDING (No. 2)

Miss Virginia Croxton

> 1 pound prunes,
> ¾ pound sugar,
> 6 eggs.

Stew, seed, and chop the prunes very fine. Beat the whites of the eggs; add the sugar, and stir in the prunes, and bake in a buttered dish for 20 minutes. Make a custard of the yolks of the eggs and 1 quart of milk. Sweeten and flavor to suit the taste. Serve the pudding in the baking-dish, and after serving in small plates, use the custard as a sauce.

RICE PUDDING (No. 1)

R. V. J.

> ½ cup of rice,
> ½ cup of sugar,
> Small piece of butter,
> 1 quart of sweet milk.

Bake slowly 4 hours, and serve with cream.

RICE PUDDING (No. 2)

Mrs. A. Moore, Jr.

2 tablespoons of rice (raw),
2 quarts of milk,
Sweetened to taste,
1 handful of seedless raisins.

Mix and pour into buttered baking-dish. Grate nutmeg on top and bake slowly until well done. When cold the pudding should be of consistency of baked custard.

Serve with cream.

SCOTCH PUDDING

Mrs. Henry C. Buckner

12 small sponge cakes, grated,
5 eggs,
1 teacup of currants,
1 teacup of raisins, cut fine,
1 teacup of sugar,
1 tablespoon of butter,
3 tablespoons of marmalade,
1 teacup of cream.

Cook 15 or 20 minutes. When pudding is nearly

done, stick it with a knife in several places, and pour over it a glass of wine. To be served with or without sauce.

SNOW PUDDING

Mrs. Ellet Cabell

Dissolve $\frac{1}{4}$ box of gelatine in 2 cups of warm water. When cold, add $\frac{1}{2}$ cup of sugar and grated peel and juice of 2 lemons. When it begins to harden, add whites of 5 eggs, well beaten. Beat thoroughly and turn into a mould. When cold, serve with a custard made of yolks of the eggs, 2 cups of milk, sugar, and flavoring to taste.

STEAMED WHITE PUDDING

E. D. P.

1 pound of flour,
2 teaspoons of baking-powder, sifted with flour,
1 pound of raisins,
$\frac{1}{2}$ pound of butter,
$\frac{1}{2}$ pound of sugar,
4 eggs,
1 cup of new milk.

Flour raisins well with some of the 1 pound of flour. Season to taste and steam 3 hours.

SUNDERLAND PUDDING

V. C. G.

6 eggs,
3 tablespoons of flour,
1 pint of sweet milk,
1 pinch of salt.

Beat the yolks well and mix smoothly with the flour. Add the milk and strain. Whip the whites to a stiff froth; beat them in, and bake immedi-ately.

TAPIOCA PUDDING

Mrs. Wash Fithian

5 tablespoons of tapioca,
1 quart of new milk,
1 tumbler of cream,
½ tumbler of wine,
4 eggs,
Flavor to taste.

Soak the tapioca in the new milk over night. Bring it to a boil and add the cream, wine, eggs (beaten separately), sugar, and flavoring.

Bake 15 or 20 minutes, and serve with a sauce.

TIPSY PARSON

R. V. J.

Moisten sponge cake with 1 cup of sherry wine. Make a custard of 1 pint of milk and yolks of 3 eggs. Pour over cake while hot.

Just before it goes to the table, stick it full of blanched almonds. Beat the whites to a stiff froth with 2 tablespoons of powdered sugar; then add 1 cup of sweet cream and pour over cake.

Before adding the last, stir in candied fruit, if desired.

VIRGINIA PLUM PUDDING

Mrs. Cyrus McCormick

1½ pounds best seeded raisins,
¾ pound finely chopped citron,
¼ pound conserved oranges,
1 pound finely shredded beef suet.
  Sift over these ingredients
1½ pounds of flour, and mix thoroughly,
Beat 6 eggs very light with 1 pound of white sugar,
Add ½ grated nutmeg,
1 wineglass of brandy,
3 teacups bread-crumbs,

234

Enough sweet milk to make a batter,
Spices to taste.

Then add 2 teaspoons of baking-powder, and lastly all the fruit. Pour in a well-greased mould or pudding-bag and boil 6 hours.

YORKSHIRE PUDDING

V. C. G.

1 pint of milk,
8 tablespoons of flour,
2 eggs,
Salt.

Mix thoroughly, so there will be no lumps, and let stand 10 or 15 minutes to get light. Take some of the gravy from the roast-beef pan and grease a small dripping-pan, leaving it about a $\frac{1}{4}$ of an inch thick on the bottom of the pan. Then pour the batter in and bake half an hour, according to oven.

Sauces for Puddings

DELICIOUS SAUCE
FOR COTTAGE PUDDING

Mrs. Joseph H. Holt

1 pint of brown sugar,
Lump of butter size of an egg,
Yolk of 1 egg.

Cream the butter, sugar, and egg together. Mix with cream and bring to a boil. Season with whisky.

FOAMING SAUCE

V. C. G.

1 cup of powdered sugar,
2 tablespoons of butter,
1 egg,
1 glass of wine.

Stir to a cream and add wineglass of wine gradually, and beat it hard till very light. Set the bowl over a teakettle of hot water till melted. Do not stir it.

HARD SAUCE

1 cup sugar,
½ cup of butter.

Cream together and flavor with lemon, wine, or brandy.

HARD SAUCE
FOR PLUM PUDDING

Cream a cup of butter and work into it 2 cups of powdered sugar. Season with 2 tablespoons French brandy and a scant teaspoon of vanilla. Beat the white of an egg and stir into it. Set on ice and serve with the hot pudding. Some prefer a mixture of whisky and rum to the brandy.

LEMON SAUCE

1 pint sugar,
1 tablespoon butter.

Pour over ½ pint hot water. Add the juice of 1 lemon. Let it boil, and add 1 tablespoon corn-starch. Strain and serve hot.

SAUCE FOR
BLUE GRASS PUDDING

$\frac{1}{4}$ pound butter,
2 cups of sugar,
2 eggs.

Mix and cook in saucepan with boiling water. Stir till it begins to thicken. When ready to serve, stir in 1 glass of brandy or whisky.

SAUCE FOR
CABINET PUDDING

E. D. P.

Cream 1 tablespoon of butter into $\frac{1}{2}$ pound of sugar. Add

Well-beaten yolks of 4 eggs,
Juice of 1 lemon, and
A little of the rind grated,
With cinnamon to taste,
$\frac{1}{2}$ teacup of wine.

Cook all together in a saucepan placed in hot water. Stir well while boiling, till thick as custard. Serve hot with pudding.

SAUCE FOR
CAKES AND PUDDINGS

Mrs. Henry C. Buckner

1 pint of brown caramel sugar,
Butter size of an egg,
Yolk of 1 egg,
½ pint of cream.

Cream butter, sugar, and egg, and add cream and boil till thick. Season with whisky or wine, if preferred.

SAUCE FOR
COCOANUT PUDDING

4 ounces of butter,
6 ounces of sugar,
1 glass of wine,
White of 1 egg.

Beat the butter and sugar till very white; add the whipped egg; then the wine; nutmeg on the top.

SAUCE (Lady Lee Pudding)

V. C. G.

1 cup of white pulverized sugar,
½ cup of butter,

1 egg,
1 wineglass of Madeira wine.

Beat all together and set in the refrigerator for
2 or 3 hours.

Just before serving, set over teakettle of boiling
water, but be careful *not* to stir it again.

VERY FINE SAUCE FOR
PLUM PUDDING

1 cup of cream,
1 cup of powdered sugar,
1 egg,
Whisky to taste.

Cream the butter till light; add the sugar; then
break an egg over it and mix thoroughly. Put
the sauce in a bowl and set in hot water. Stir till
it melts and add the whisky and serve.

Cakes

ALMOND WAFERS

Mrs. Henry C. Buckner

1 tablespoonful of powdered sugar,
½ saltspoonful of salt.

Stir well together. Beat white of 1 egg just enough to break it; add enough flour to sugar to make it creamy. Flavor with a few drops of bitter almond essence. Grease the pan lightly and flour. Drop ½ teaspoonful of the paste on the pan, and with a wet finger spread into a thin round wafer. Bake in a moderate oven till the edges are lightly browned; then before removing from the oven door, lift each wafer and turn round a stick.

ANGEL'S FOOD CAKE

Miss Annie White

Whites of 12 eggs,
10 ounces icing sugar,

$3\frac{1}{2}$ ounces flour,
1 teaspoon vanilla,
1 teaspoon cream of tartar.

Sift flour 5 times; add cream of tartar and sift again. Sift sugar 3 times. Beat eggs very light; add sugar, vanilla, and flour last, stirred in very lightly. Bake 50 or 60 minutes. When done, do not take out of mould till cold. The mould should be greased only on the bottom. When taken out of the oven it must be turned upside down on something to let the air to it.

BLACK CAKE (No. 1)

Mrs. John W. Fox

1 pound flour,
1 pound sugar, sifted,
1 pound butter,
12 eggs, beaten separately,
2 nutmegs,
1 small teacup of blackberry jam,
1 cup of dark molasses,
2 cups of brandy or whisky,
2 pounds raisins,
2 pounds currants,
$\frac{1}{2}$ pound citron,

1 tablespoon cloves,
2 tablespoons cinnamon,
1 tablespoon mace,
1 tablespoon allspice,
¼ pound figs, chopped fine,
½ cup of nuts,
1 small cup vinegar,
1 teaspoon soda,
½ pound candied orange.

Put the flour in a bread-pan and brown to a dark color. Do not burn it. Beat the eggs separately, then together. Cut the citron in very thin slices and dredge with flour. Dredge the fruits with flour and chop the figs and crush the nuts. Beat the butter and sugar to a cream, and add eggs alternately with the flour. Add molasses, jam, brandy, and spices, and then the nuts. Stir the fruits in lightly, and just before putting in the pan, add the vinegar, in which the teaspoon soda is stirred, and pour foaming into the mixture. Put in a layer of the mixture, then sprinkle the citron over it, then another layer, and so on, but do not put any on top. Bake slowly for 4 hours or longer. When cold, cover with icing flavored with a little citric acid.

BLACK CAKE (No. 2)

Mrs. Henry C. Buckner

1   pound of browned flour,
1   pound of sugar,
1¼ pounds of butter,
13 eggs,
4   pounds of raisins,
2   pounds of currants,
1   pound of citron,
½ pint of whisky,
1   nutmeg,
1   teaspoon of cinnamon,
½ teaspoon of mace,
½ teaspoon of cloves,
1   pint of acid cherry preserves.

Just before putting in the oven, stir in a small teacup of vinegar with 1 teaspoon of soda.

Bake 4 or 5 hours in a moderate oven.

BLACKBERRY CAKE

Mrs. Mary E. Goddard

3   eggs,
1   cup of sugar,
¾ cup of butter,

246

CORN DODGERS

BEATEN BISCUIT

1½ cups of flour,
1   cup of blackberry jam *or* preserves,
3   tablespoons of sour cream,
1   teaspoon of cinnamon,
1   teaspoon of allspice,
1   teaspoon of soda,
1   nutmeg.

Mix well and bake in layers, and spread white icing betweeen.

BLUE GRASS PLUM CAKE

R. V. J.

1   pound of butter,
1   pound of granulated sugar,
1   pound of flour,
1   dozen eggs (white and yellows well beaten separately),
3   pounds of raisins (after seeding),
1½ pounds of currants (after cleaning),
1½ pounds of citron (cut very thin),
1   nutmeg (grated),
2   tablespoons of powdered cinnamon,
1½ pounds of blanched almonds (sliced),

247

1½ pounds of candied fruit (cut in small pieces),
    cherries, peaches, or apricots (do not cut
    cherries),
2   lemons (juice),
1   cup of golden syrup,
1   tumbler of mixed brandy, whisky, or rum.

Flour all the fruit with part of 1 pound called
for, and do not add extra flour.

Bake slowly in moderate oven for 5 or 6 hours.

BLUE GRASS WHITE CAKE

Mrs. John C. Berryman

Whites of 12 eggs,
1   tumbler of butter,
2½ tumblers of sugar,
3½ tumblers of flour, after sifting,
 ⅓ teaspoon of soda, sifted with flour,
1   teaspoon of cream of tartar.

Bake in mould or bread-pan for 1 hour.

CARAMEL LAYER CAKE

Whites of 4 eggs,
1 cup of butter,
1 cup of sugar,

½ cup of milk,
½ pound of flour,
1 teaspoon of baking-powder sifted with the flour.

Mix sugar and butter to a cream; then add milk, eggs, and flour. Flavor with vanilla, and bake in layers.

Filling:

>2 cups good brown sugar,
>1 cup of cream,
>1 tablespoon butter.

Put in granite kettle, and when it begins to boil add 1 tablespoonful of caramel (burnt brown sugar). Boil till thick. Take from stove and beat till it thickens. Flavor with vanilla; then spread between layers and on top. Cover the top with English walnuts.

CHOCOLATE LAYER CAKE

Whites of 3 eggs,
1 cup of cream or rich milk,
3 cups flour, sifted with 2 teaspoons baking-powder,
2 large tablespoons butter.

Cream the butter and sugar; then add flour and cream. Add the eggs last, and flavor with a little vanilla. Bake in jelly-pans, and when nearly cool put a filling between them and on top.

Filling:

> 2 cups brown sugar,
> ½ cake Baker's chocolate.

Cover with milk and add a tablespoon of butter. Cook till thick. Flavor with vanilla, and spread on cakes while warm.

CRULLERS

E. D. P.

1 cup of sugar,
½ cup of butter,
1 cup of sweet milk,
2 teaspoons of baking-powder,
Nutmeg, cinnamon, or rose water to taste,
3 eggs,
Flour enough to make a stiff dough.

Beat the yolks very light; add sugar, butter; then milk, with flour for stiff dough. Add seasoning and the whites well beaten. At the last, add baking-powder. Roll, cut in shapes, and fry rich brown in hot lard.

DEVIL'S FOOD CAKE

Miss Bashford

4   ounces of chocolate,
½ pint of milk,
½ cup of butter,
1½ cups of sugar,
4   eggs,
3   cups of flour,
2   teaspoonfuls of baking-powder.

Put chocolate in milk and cook in double-boiler till smooth and thick (about 5 minutes), and stand aside to cool. Beat the butter to a cream, and add gradually the sugar and yolks of eggs; then the cold chocolate mixture, and add the flour, which has been sifted with the baking-powder. Add the well-beaten whites of eggs and flavor with vanilla. Bake in layers and put together with soft icing, to which add chopped figs or nuts.

DOUGHNUTS

Mrs. H. C. McDowell

1 egg,
1 cup of rich milk,

1 cup of sugar,
3 pints of flour,
3 teaspoons baking-powder,
1 teaspoon melted butter.

Beat the egg well and then add the milk and sugar, stirring constantly; then the butter and flour last, with the baking-powder. Roll out on bread-boards as quickly and as lightly as possible. Fry in hot lard and sprinkle with sugar.

EXCELLENT DOUGHNUTS

Mrs. W. W. Massie

2 eggs, beaten together,
2 tablespoons of fine lard (not melted),
1 coffeecup of granulated sugar,
½ pint of milk (skimmed),
Enough flour to make a soft dough,
1 heaping teaspoon of Royal baking-powder, sifted in flour.

Roll out, cut in shape, and fry in boiling lard. When cold, dust them in pulverized sugar, to which a small quantity of pulverized cinnamon is added.

RAISED DOUGHNUTS

Mrs. Cyrus McCormick

> 1 pint sweet milk,
> ½ pint lard,
> 1 pint sugar,
> 3 eggs.

Mix soft at night, using the milk, one-half the sugar and lard, ½ pint yeast. In the morning, add the rest with the eggs, 1 nutmeg, 2 tablespoons whisky, and a little soda. Knead well and set to rise. When light roll out thin, and after cutting let rise again before frying.

EXCELLENT MARBLE CAKE

White part:

> Whites of 7 eggs,
> 3 teacups sugar,
> 1 teacup of butter,
> 4 teacups flour,
> 1 teacup sour cream,
> ½ teaspoon soda in cream,
> 1 teaspoon of cream of tartar in flour.

Cream sugar and butter. Add cream; then flour and eggs alternately. Flavor to taste and bake in layers.

Dark part:

Yolks of 7 eggs,
2 teacups of brown sugar,
1 teacup of molasses,
1 teacup butter,
5 teacups flour,
1 teacup of sour cream,
1 teaspoon soda in cream,
Spices to taste.

Bake in layers, and stack alternate layers of dark and white together with white icing, flavored with lemon.

FRUIT CAKE

R. V. J.

1 pound of butter,
1 pound of sugar,
12 eggs,
1 pound of flour,
$\frac{1}{2}$ gill of brandy,
1 nutmeg,
$\frac{1}{2}$ teaspoon of cloves,
2 teaspoons of cinnamon,
1$\frac{1}{2}$ pounds of raisins,
1$\frac{1}{4}$ pounds of currants,
1 pound of citron.

Seed the raisins; slice the citron in thin slices. Beat butter and sugar to a cream. Beat the eggs together till thick, then add them by degrees; also flour, brandy, spices, and the fruits last, and $\frac{1}{2}$ teacup of golden syrup. Line the pan, rub with butter, and bake in a moderate oven about 4 hours.

WHITE FRUIT CAKE

Miss Elise White

1 pound sugar,
1 pound flour,
$\frac{3}{4}$ pound butter,
Whites of 12 eggs,
2 pounds citron,
2 pounds almonds,
1 large cocoanut, grated.

Add 1 tablespoon of soda and 2 of cream of tartar to flour and sift. Cream butter and sugar, and then add eggs, which have been beaten separately, and add flour alternately with whites. Beat well; then add lightly one-half of fruit, and put remainder in layers with the mixture in cake-mould. Bake slowly and carefully. Have almonds blanched and cut, and citron mixed with flour, cut in thin strips; cocoanut grated.

FRUIT COOKIES

Mrs. Henry C. Buckner

Beat well together

    3 cups of brown sugar,
    1 cup of butter,
    1 cup of sour milk,
    1 teaspoon of soda,
    4 eggs, well beaten,
    1 teaspoon of cloves,
    2 teaspoons of cinnamon,
    1 teaspoon of nutmeg,
    2 cups of seeded and chopped raisins.

Flour enough to make a stiff batter that will drop off a spoon.   Bake in a quick oven.

1 teacup of nuts would be an improvement.

FRUIT AND DELICATE CAKE

Mrs. Henry C. Buckner

    2½ cups of sugar,
    4½ cups of flour, sifted,
    1 cup of butter,
    1 cup of sour milk,
    1 teaspoon of soda, not heaped,
    4 eggs.

Flavor with lemon; fill 3 jelly tins. Then add to the remainder

> 1 cup of chopped raisins,
> 1 cup of currants,
> ½ citron,
> 2 tablespoons of molasses,
> 1 tablespoon of brandy,
> 1 tablespoon of cinnamon,
> ½ tablespoon of mace or allspice.

After it is baked, put alternate layers of light and dark with thick icing.

SOFT GINGER BREAD (No. 1)

V. C. G.

1 large coffeecup of sugar,
1 large coffeecup of molasses,
1 large coffeecup of butter,
4 large coffeecups of flour,
1 large coffeecup of sour milk,
4 eggs,
½ teacup of ginger,
½ teaspoon of ground cloves,
½ teaspoon of cinnamon,
1 tablespoon of saleratus beaten into the sour milk, and poured in last.

SOFT GINGER BREAD (No. 2)

1½ cups of brown sugar,
1   cup of butter,
2   eggs,
1   teaspoon of soda, dissolved in a cup of butter-
    milk,
2   cups of sifted flour,
1   cup of dark molasses,
2   more cups of flour,
4   tablespoons of ginger.

Mix in the order written.

JUMBLES

Miss Elise White

6 eggs,
1 pound sugar,
¾ pound butter.

Cream butter and sugar, beat the eggs into it with just enough flour to roll out. Take small quantity of dough and lay on board, and with a knife roll in sugar and flour.

258

DROP JUMBLES

Mrs. Henry C. Buckner

1   pound of sugar,
1   pound of butter,
1¼ pounds of flour,
Juice of fresh lemon to taste,
8   eggs, beaten separately.

Use 2 heaping teaspoons of baking-powder in the flour, and sift several times. Have your pans well greased, and dip a teaspoon of batter at a time a little distance apart.

KENTUCKY CAKE

Mrs. Joseph H. Holt

12 eggs (whites)
1   pound of flour,
1   pound of sugar,
¾   pound of butter,
1   pound of raisins,
1   heaping teaspoon of baking-powder,
1   wineglass of whisky with a little nutmeg grated
      into it.

Wash butter and then cream it very light with sugar. Beat whites to stiff froth. Add alter-

259

nately with the flour, reserving 1 small cup of flour to mix with baking-powder. Next, put in whisky and raisins, and lastly, sift in the cup of flour and baking-powder.

Bake 2 hours in slow oven.

MOUNTAIN CAKE
V. C. G.

½   teacup of butter,
½   teacup of cornstarch,
½   teacup of sweet milk,
1½ teacups of sugar,
1½ teacups of flour,
1   teaspoon of cream of tartar,
½   teaspoon of soda,
1   teaspoon of vanilla,
Whites of 5 eggs.

Bake in jelly pans and make 5 layers.

FROSTING FOR SAME

15 tablespoons of pulverized sugar,
1   grated cocoanut,
Whites of 5 eggs.

Beat the whites of eggs nearly stiff before adding the sugar. Spread on each layer, and sprinkle cocoanut over and on top and sides.

MRS. HENRY CLAY'S DROP CAKES

4 eggs,
6 ounces of butter,
8 ounces of sugar,
8 ounces of flour.

OLD VIRGINIA CHRISTMAS CAKE

12 eggs,
1 pound flour,
1 pound sugar,
1 pound butter,
1 nutmeg,
1 teaspoon each of mace and cinnamon,
3 pounds of raisins,
3 pounds currants,
½ pound citron,
1 pound each of cream nuts and almonds,
½ pint of brandy,
½ teaspoon soda in small cup of vinegar. Put in last.

Bake 3 or 4 hours. Cover with icing made of eggs and sugar. Flavor with acid.

PECAN CAKE (No. 1)

E. D. P.

1½ pounds of brown sugar,
1 teacup of molasses,
1 pound of flour,
⅓ pound of butter,
6 eggs (beaten separately),
1 pound of pecans after they are shelled,
1½ pounds of raisins,
½ nutmeg, grated,
1 wineglass of whisky.

Bake about 3 hours.

PECAN CAKE (No. 2)

E. D. P.

1 pound of sugar,
1 pound of flour,
⅓ pound of butter,
2 pounds of pecans, before picking,
1½ pounds of raisins,
½ nutmeg,
1 tumbler of whisky or brandy,
6 eggs, beaten separately,
1 teaspoon of baking-powder.

POMMES DE TERRE

Mrs. R. H. Hanson

1 pound blanched almonds,
1 pound powdered sugar,
Pound the almonds to a paste.

Beat the whites of 2 eggs very light and mix in the almonds and sugar till smooth and flavor with rose and vanilla. Cut the cake in small pieces, shape like an Irish potato, and roll the paste around the cake, then roll in powdered sugar or powdered cinnamon.

POUND CAKE (No. 1)

E. D. P.

1 pound of flour,
1 pound of butter,
1 pound of sugar,
10 eggs.

Cream butter well, then sugar till very light. Beat eggs till light, velvety, and thick. Add 2 wineglasses of liquor—any kind preferred, then flour and eggs alternately.

POUND CAKE (No. 2)

An Old-Time Recipe

12 eggs,
1 pound butter,
1 pound sugar,
1 pound flour.

Cream the butter and add the flour. Beat the yolks, and add to them the sugar, then add to the butter and last the frothed whites. Beat well and flavor with brandy or whisky. Bake in a papered mould in a moderate oven. The old-fashioned way was to bake this recipe in teacups and ice them with white icing, and they were called " Snowballs."

ROBERT LEE JELLY CAKE

Use any recipe for sponge layer cake and fill with the following:

Yolks of 3 eggs,
Juice and grated rind of 1 lemon,
$\frac{1}{4}$ pound of butter,
$\frac{1}{2}$ pound of sugar.

Put in a skillet on the stove and stir till cooked; then put in the well-beaten 3 whites. As soon as it

comes to a boil, take off and stir till cold.   Put
between layers of cake.

SIMPLE WHITE CUP CAKE

Miss Annie Lyle

>5 eggs,
>1 cup of butter,
>1 cup of milk,
>3 cups of flour after sifting,
>2 cups of sugar,
>2 teaspoons baking-powder.

SPICE CAKE

Miss Annie White

4 teacups flour,
1 good teacup of butter,
3 teacups sugar,
4 eggs,
1 teaspoon soda in 1 cup of sour milk or cream,
$\frac{1}{2}$ tablespoon each of nutmeg, allspice, mace, cin-
>namon, and cloves.

Cream butter and sugar.   Break the 4 eggs over
it and beat.   Add milk and soda, and put in gradually flour and the spices.   Drop with spoon in
pans and ice with white icing and flavor with lemon.

ALLEGHANY TEA CAKES

1 pound butter,
1 pound sugar,
8 eggs,
1¼ pounds flour.

Rub butter and sugar together, and add by degrees the well-beaten eggs and the flour. Flavor to taste. Drop with spoon on well-greased tin pans.

GERMAN TEA CAKES

Mrs. W. W. Massie

Hard-boiled yolks of 10 eggs, rubbed finely
    through a sieve,
2 raw eggs, beaten,
1 pound of butter,
1 pound of sugar,
1 tablespoon of whisky,
Flour enough to make a very soft dough.

Sprinkle sugar over each rolling of dough. Cut in fancy shapes.

TEA CAKES (No. 1)

Mrs. H. C. McDowell

4 eggs beaten separately,
1 teacup of lard,
2 heaping teacups of brown sugar,
1 scant half cup of sour milk in which dissolve 2
    level teaspoons of soda,
1 grated nutmeg,
1 teaspoon lemon extract,
Flour enough to roll out.

Bake in rather hot oven.

TEA CAKES (No. 2)

Miss Virginia Croxton

1 quart flour,
6 ounces butter,
¾ pound sugar,
3 eggs,
2 heaping teaspoons baking-powder.

Flavor with vanilla or cinnamon. Roll out about
¼ inch thick, cut in shapes, and bake in a quick
oven.

267

TIP-TOP CAKE

2 eggs,

1½ cups sugar,

1 teaspoonful of soda dissolved in 1 cup of sweet milk,

2½ cups flour,

2 teaspoonfuls of cream of tartar,

2 tablespoonfuls of melted butter. Flavor to taste.

Cream sugar and butter, and then add beaten eggs, flour, etc., and bake in layers.

VELVET SPONGE CAKE

6 eggs,

2 cups sugar,

1 cup of boiling water,

3 cups flour,

1 tablespoon baking-powder.

Separate the eggs and beat the yolks and add to them the sugar and beat till very light. Add the whites, then the hot water, and last, beat the flour in very lightly. Put together with icing and flavor with lemon. This recipe makes a nice cake baked in a big mould or in layers or in muffin rings. Bake in a moderate oven.

VENETIAN CAKE

Mrs. Henry C. Buckner

½ cupful of butter,
½ cupful of powdered sugar,
1½ cupfuls of flour,
1 teaspoonful of vanilla,
½ cupful of almonds,
Yolks of 3 eggs.

Cream butter and sugar very light; add yolks well-beaten, the almonds cut; mix and add vanilla and stir in lightly the flour. The dough should be rather soft. Take a small piece at a time, drop into powdered sugar, roll in the hands in a ball an inch in diameter. Put a piece of pistachio nut on the top. Place the balls a little distance apart on a floured pan, and bake in a moderate oven 10 or 15 minutes. They will look like macaroons.

WASHINGTON CAKE

V. C. G.

1 pound of flour,
1 pound of brown sugar,
½ pound of butter,
1 cup of sweet milk,

1 teaspoon of soda, sifted with flour,
1 pound of raisins, stoned,
½ pound of currants,
½ pound of citron,
1 cup of English walnuts, chopped fine,
4 eggs, beaten together,
1 teaspoon of cinnamon,
1 teaspoon of cloves,
½ glass of whisky.

Bake in a 4-quart can, and in a slow oven.

WHITE CAKE

Mrs. Simms

1 large teacup of butter,
2 large teacups of sugar,
3 large teacups of flour,
Whites of 12 eggs,
2 heaping teaspoons of baking-powder,
1 cup of sweet milk.

If large mould is used, put in 2 cups of seeded raisins. Mix sugar and butter night before. Add flour and whites alternately—milk last, then ½ cup of flour with the baking-powder in it.

WHITE SPONGE CAKE (No. 1)

Mrs. J. C. Berryman

Whites of 12 eggs beaten very light. Beat in ¾ pound of sugar, then stir, and put in slowly ½ pound of flour, a little at a time.

Bake in pan ½ hour.

WHITE SPONGE CAKE (No. 2)

R. V. G.

13 eggs, whites only,
4 yolks,
1 pound of sugar,
½ pound of flour,
1 lemon.

Beat the yolks and sugar together till very light. Then add the whites, which have been well beaten, and beat all together well. Cut in the flour with a knife, and add juice of lemon.

Bake *very* slowly an hour and a half in a large-sized mould.

Fillings for Cakes

ALMOND FILLING (No. 1)

1 cup of sour cream, heated to boiling point,
Stir into it 3 teaspoons cornstarch,
Yolks of 3 eggs, beaten with 1 cup of sugar,
Beat the whites to a stiff froth and add last,
1 teacup of almonds after they are shelled.

Blanch them and roll fine. Return the mixture to the fire and stir constantly till thick.

ALMOND ICING (No. 2)

Miss Mary Bashford

1   pound of almonds,
3   cups of white sugar,
1½ cups of sweet cream,
4   tablespoons of butter.

Boil till it is a soft jelly. Remove from the stove and flavor with extract of almond. Blanch the almonds, dry them thoroughly, and then grind or grate them nicely, reserving a few for the top of cake. Stir them in the icing and spread on the cake, and ornament top with almonds in halves.

FINE ALMOND FILLING FOR CAKE (No. 3)

Mrs. R. H. Hanson

2 pounds almonds,
1 cup sugar,
1 cup sour cream.

Blanch and pulverize the almonds and add sugar and cream. Color with a little cochineal. Add a little more sugar and cream if not sweet and thin enough.

BOILED ICING

Whites of 3 eggs,
3 cups of white sugar,
Water enough to dissolve.

Pour the water over the sugar and let it cook till it is thick, or the syrup threads when dropped from a spoon. Beat the whites of the eggs to a stiff froth and pour the syrup over them, beating all the time. Use any flavor desired. When it begins to thicken, spread on cakes with a broad knife. If the icing hardens, heat the knife through in hot water and it can be spread on perfectly smooth on top and sides.

CARAMEL ICING

R. V. J.

2 coffeecups of light-brown sugar,
½ cup of butter,
½ cup of cream.

Cook ½ hour, stirring all the time to prevent burning. Pour on a platter and stir until cool enough to spread between cakes.

Nuts chopped fine are a nice addition to the icing.

CHOCOLATE ICING

V. C. G.

Use one-half cake of Baker's chocolate, and put in sufficient water to dissolve it and boil, stirring all the time. When cold, take the yolks of 3 eggs, ½ cup of cream or milk, sweeten to taste, and boil all till quite thick. Spread between layers and on top of cake.

COCOANUT FILLING

Follow the recipe for boiled icing; spread on cakes with fresh, grated cocoanut sprinkled thick on each layer on top and sides.

FRUIT FILLING

Mrs. R. H. Hanson

1 pound almonds in the shell,
½ pound raisins,
¼ pound citron,
¼ pound figs.

Blanch almonds and cut into 2 or 3 small pieces. Scald and clip raisins and cut figs and citron into small pieces. For icing, use 3 eggs and 3 cups sugar. Flavor with rose and stir in fruit. In making icing, put 3 cups of white sugar into pan and cover with water and let boil till thick, then pour over the well-beaten whites of three eggs, whipping all the time, and when thick put quickly between cakes.

FILLINGS FOR CAKES

LEMON FILLING

Miss Mary Bashford

6 eggs, beaten separately,
3 lemons, grated rind of 2,
¾ teacup of ice water.

Sweeten to taste. Cook in vessel of hot water until thick. Spread on cake.

LEMON JELLY FOR CAKE

1½ cups of powdered sugar,
Juice of 2 lemons,
2 eggs.

Mix sugar and lemon juice and beaten eggs, cook over hot water until it thickens like soft custard. Don't stir after taking from fire.

MARSHMALLOW FILLING

Use boiled icing, and when thick enough to spread flavor with marshmallows dissolved in the icing. Cut marshmallows into halves or quarters, and spread on each layer. Pour icing over each. Place whole marshmallows on top and cover with icing.

NUT FILLING

Use recipe for boiled icing, and when ready to spread on cake, sprinkle chopped nuts and raisins on each layer and pour icing over. Decorate top and sides with whole kernels stuck in soft icing. Flavor with bitter almond.

PRALINE ICING

Miss Mary Bashford

1½ cups of shelled pecan nuts,
2½ cups of sugar,
1   cup of maple syrup,
1   cup of cream.

Boil till thick and flavor with vanilla. When thick enough to spread on cakes, add 1 cup of nuts and put between layers. Decorate top with kernels.

WHITE CREAM CARAMEL FILLING

Miss Mary Bashford

3   cups of white sugar,
1½ cups of thick, sweet cream,

4   tablespoons of sweet butter,
1   teacup of almonds, blanched and grated.

Flavor with extract of almond. Stir well together and boil till it is thick. Take off the fire and let it stand for a few minutes. Beat till it is thick, and spread on cakes.

Beverages

BLUE GRASS APPLE TODDY

Dissolve 2 lumps of sugar in 1 ounce of hot water. Add a hot baked apple and 1½ ounces of good high-proof old Kentucky whisky.

HOT APPLE TODDY
Virginia Recipe

Roast (not bake) thoroughly 1 dozen medium-sized juicy apples. (Winesaps, pippins, or other sub-acid juicy varieties preferred.) Scrape the pulp and juice (free from skin, core, and seeds). Put into a bowl, add 1 pound of granulated or pulverized sugar and stir thoroughly.

Add 1 quart best whisky and ½ pint Jamaica rum. Stir again thoroughly. This is the pug and may be kept for almost any time.

Serve steaming hot (from chafing-dish) in glass

punch cups with handles, adding as served boiling water $\frac{1}{4}$ or $\frac{1}{3}$ the amount of pug. (Use tea or bouillon spoons, not after-dinner coffee-spoons.)

The water should be added with extreme caution.

OLD-FASHIONED KENTUCKY TODDY

$\frac{1}{4}$ glass of water,
$\frac{1}{4}$ glass of good whisky,
2 lumps of loaf sugar.

Dissolve sugar in water thoroughly, add whisky and 1 lump of ice, not crushed, as it melts rapidly and spoils proportions of drink.

BOURBON WHISKY PUNCH

E. D. P.

Squeeze 10 lemons and stir the juice in 3 pints of water. Add 1 quart of Jamaica rum and 1 gallon of Bourbon whisky and sweeten to taste. Let it simmer slowly for 20 minutes. Cover till cold and then bottle. Drink either cold or hot, and add water if too strong.

CHERRY SHRUB

To 1 pint of juice add ¼ pound sugar,
Brandy to taste.

Put the cherries in a stone jar and set in kettle
of cold water. Let the water boil till the cherries
burst, strain, sweeten, and add the brandy. Bottle
till ready to use.

CHOCOLATE (No. 1)

E. D. P.

In making chocolate, put a little warm water
over the broken pieces of chocolate and let it stand
till soft. Boil 1 pint of milk and 1 pint of cream,
and add to the chocolate. Use 4 or 5 squares, according to taste. Boil well for 10 minutes and beat
well till frothy. Serve immediately.

If cream can not be had, use all new milk.

CHOCOLATE (No. 2)

Mrs. J. W. Fox

To 6 cups of chocolate allow a tablespoon of
pulverized chocolate to each cup. Put the chocolate in a cup of hot water and let it come to a boil
and skim off the oil that rises. Put 6 cups of cream

or rich milk on and boil (1 cup to a tablespoon of chocolate) and when it boils add chocolate and 2 tablespoons of sugar. Serve with whipped cream and add sugar to taste.

HOT CHOCOLATE (No. 3)

Miss Virginia Croxton

> 3 ounces chocolate,
> 2 teaspoons cornstarch,
> 1 quart milk,
> 1 quart water,
> ½ pound sugar.

Melt chocolate and starch and add sugar and 1 pint milk. Let it boil up once, then add rest of milk and water and boil 20 minutes. If wanted very good and rich, add 2 beaten eggs with last milk.

CLARET CUP

Mrs. Campbell Carrington Cochran

> 3 quarts of claret,
> 3 bottles of soda water,
> 6 lemons, cut very thin,
> 1 cup of sugar.

Just before serving, add large piece of ice to cool it.

COFFEE (No. 1)

Mrs. J. W. Fox

Allow a tablespoonful of ground coffee for each cup, and 1 extra spoonful for good measure. For 6 cups take 7 tablespoons of coffee and stir into it the white of 1 egg and ½ cup of cold water. To each spoonful add 1 cup of boiling water and let all boil 10 minutes. Pour off and serve.

Use only the best fresh-roasted coffee; 1 pound of Java to ⅓ of Mocha make a good combination.

COFFEE (No. 2)

E. D. P.

⅓ Mocha,
⅔ Java,
Roast well.

Allow 2 heaping tablespoons to 1 pint of water. Scald the pot; put coffee in with the white of an egg, beat well. Add 1 tablespoon of cold water to moisten coffee well. Pour on boiling water and let it boil 12 minutes, stirring the grounds down first when it boils up. Pour out 1 cupful to see if it is clear, and pour back in pot. Throw in ½ cup of cold water and let it stand 5 minutes, and then pour off the grounds.

For after-dinner coffee use 2½ spoons of coffee to 1 pint of water.

EGG-NOG

E. D. P.

1 quart of cream,
Yolks of 4 eggs,
5 tablespoons of sugar,
5 wineglasses of liquor (say 3 of good whisky and 2 of Jamaica rum),
Nutmeg to taste.

Beat the cream to a stiff froth. The yolks are beaten very light and the sugar is added. Let this stand till the liquor cooks the eggs, then stir in the cream.

VERY FINE EGG-NOG

R. V. J.

1 gallon of cream,
24 eggs, using only the yolks,
26 tablespoons of sugar,
½ grated nutmeg,
8 wineglasses of rum,

10 wineglasses of brandy,
8 wineglasses of whisky.

Beat the eggs till *very* light, adding the sugar as you beat, then add the liquor, beating all well together. Then add the cream, except 1 quart, which whip to a stiff froth, and stir in gradually and lightly. Add the nutmeg.

After adding the liquor to the eggs, it is well to let it stand for a while before adding the cream, as it cooks the eggs.

KENTUCKY CATAWBA PUNCH

3 bottles of Catawba wine,
6 lemons,
4 oranges,
1 glass of brandy,
½ pound sugar.

KENTUCKY CHAMPAGNE PUNCH

1 bottle of champagne,
½ pint of sugar,
1 wineglass rum,
4 lemons,
2 oranges.

287

PENDENNIS CLUB MINT JULEP

By a well-known member of the club, Louisville, Ky.

These are some essentials:

1st. Fine, straight, old Kentucky Bourbon whisky—blended whiskies do not give good results.

2d. An abundant supply of freshly cut sprigs of mint—preferably young shoots—no portion of which has been bruised.

3d. Dry, cracked flint ice. A glass will answer the purpose, but a silver mug is preferable. At this club, silver cups are kept on ice. A syrup of sugar and water is also kept on hand.

The silver cup is first filled with the ice, and then the desired quantity of fine whisky poured in and thoroughly shaken with a spoon or shaker until a heavy frost forms on the mug. The desired amount of syrup is then poured in and stirred enough to be mixed. The mint is then carefully placed in the mugs with the stems barely sticking in the ice and the tops projecting 2 inches above the top of the cup. Straws are then placed in the cup, reaching from the bottom to about 1 inch above the top, and the sooner one sticks one's nose

in the mint and begins drinking through the
straws the better. There is no flavor of mint,
merely the odor.

Any stinting in quality or *quantity* materially
affects the result.

PUNCH (No. 1)

1 quart claret,
1 pint sherry,
½ dozen lemons,
8–10 oranges,
1 can pineapple,
½ pint whisky,
(Champagne, if you like.)

If served frozen, add claret, sherry, whisky, and
champagne after it is frozen.

PUNCH (No. 2)
E. D. P.

1 pint of green tea,
1 gallon of lemonade,
1 quart of French brandy,
1 quart of Jamaica rum.

When ready to serve, add thin slices of lemon
and 2 bottles of champagne.

289

PUNCH À LA REGENT
E. D. P.

1 quart bottle of dry champagne,
1 pint of good whisky,
1 quart of well-drawn tea,
1 tumblerful of Maraschino cordial,
1 wineglass of good rum,
8 thin slices of pineapple,
4 tablespoons of granulated sugar,
The rind and juice of 1 lemon,
The rind and juice of 1 orange.

Mix brandy, champagne, and rum together. Peel and cut in thin slices the pineapple, also rinds of lemon and orange. Strain the juice and add all to the champagne, etc. Add Maraschino cordial and green tea last.

This can be put in wide-mouthed bottles and kept for weeks on ice. In drinking it use ice freely. Water can be added, should it prove too strong for some tastes.

ROMAN PUNCH
E. D. P.

½ gallon of water,
6 lemons, juice,
1 teacup of rum.

Strain the lemon juice and water, and sweeten to taste. Make very sweet to allow for rum. Freeze, and just before sending to table, stir in the rum.

SHERRY COBBLER

3 lemons,
3 oranges,
6 slices of ripe pineapple,
1 large cup of powdered sugar.

Slice the fruits very thin and put them in a bowl or pitcher, cover with the sugar and crushed ice and let it stand for 15 or 20 minutes. Then pour over it 2 large glasses of water. Add more crushed ice and season highly with sherry. Serve in glasses with slices of the fruit and strawberries.

TOM AND JERRY

1 dozen eggs,
1 tablespoon sugar,
1 tablespoon ground cloves,
1 tablespoon allspice,
1½ tablespoons cinnamon,
1 wineglass of Jamaica rum.

Beat the eggs separately. Mix the sugar with the yolks, then add the whites. Add the spices and rum last.

To serve it take:

1 tablespoon of mixture and add 1 wineglass of old whisky and same amount of hot water. Grate a little nutmeg on top and serve.

The mixture will keep many days.

XALAPA PUNCH

½ gallon of strong tea,
Grated rind of 1 lemon.

Let it stand a few minutes and strain.

Add 1 pound of loaf sugar.

Equal parts of Syracuse rum, apple brandy, and claret wine to suit the taste.

Serve with ice and thinly sliced lemon.

Brandied Peaches

BRANDIED PEACHES (No. 1)

Mrs. Henry C. Buckner

12 pounds of fruit,
6 pounds of white sugar.

Sprinkle sugar on the fruit and let it stand 6 hours. Then boil till fruit is tender. Add 1 ounce of peach-stones to boiling mixture. When cold, add peach brandy to taste.

BRANDIED PEACHES (No. 2)

Mrs. John W. Fox

Pour hot boiling water over white clingstone peaches and rub the peeling off. Make a rich syrup of half a pound of sugar to a pound of fruit. Add water to sugar, and when the syrup boils up, drop the peaches in and let them cook till the fruit can be pierced with a straw. Remove the peaches and put in a jar. Let the syrup boil till very thick, and while warm add an equal part of brandy and pour over the fruit. Seal in glass jars. Ready for use at any time.

VERY FINE
BRANDIED PEACHES

E. D. P.

5 pounds of ripe clingstone peaches, after peeling,
5 pounds of granulated sugar.

Keep cover on top of kettle and boil till clear. Lift peaches out and drain well through a sifter. Keep covered and boil the syrup till it is like thick maple syrup. Remove from stove and let it cool. After peaches have drained well, put in glass jars. To each pint of syrup add 1 pint of good peach brandy. Stir and pour well over the peaches in jars.

If there is more syrup than needed, bottle for *Peach Cordial.*

Wines

BLACKBERRY CORDIAL

Mrs. John W. Fox

Mash and strain the berries through a sieve.
> To 1 gallon of juice,
> Put 1 pound of sugar.

Boil and add
> 1 tablespoon of allspice,
> 1 tablespoon of cloves.

Cook till thick. When nearly cold add
> 1 quart of whisky or brandy.

Bottle and seal.

BLACKBERRY WINE

Bruise the berries well with the hands.
To 1 gallon of fruit add ½ gallon of water, and let it stand over night. Strain and measure, and to each gallon of juice add 2½ pounds sugar. Put in cask and let ferment. Tack thin muslin over

top, and when fermentation stops, pour into jugs or kegs.

Wine keeps best in kegs.

STRAWBERRY WINE

Mrs. John W. Fox

Crush the berries and add 1 quart of water to a gallon of berries and let it stand 24 hours. Strain and add 2½ pounds of white sugar to a gallon of juice. Put in a cask, with thin muslin tacked over the bunghole, and let it ferment, keeping it full from a quantity reserved for the purpose. If a small quantity is made, use jugs or bottle. When fermentation ceases, add 1 pint of good whisky to the gallon, and bottle and seal securely. Ready for use in six weeks.

GRAPE WINE

Crush the grapes and let them stand 1 week. Draw off the juice, strain; add 1 quart of water and 3 pounds of sugar to each gallon. Put in a barrel or cask, with a thin piece of muslin tacked over the bunghole, and let it stand till fermentation stops. Put in a cask and seal securely and let it stand for six months. Then bottle and seal and keep in a cool place.

Pickles

BLUE GRASS
GREEN TOMATO PICKLE

E. D. P.

1   peck of green tomatoes,
2   dozen onions,
2   tablespoons of mustard,
2   tablespoons of black pepper,
1   lemon,
2   tablespoons of turmeric,
3½ pounds of best brown sugar,
2   ounces of white mustard seed,
2   ounces of celery seed,
3   pods of red pepper,
3   pints of vinegar,
1   teaspoon of ground cloves,
1   teaspoon of allspice.

Slice tomatoes and onions and cover with salt and let stand over night. Squeeze well through a cloth; put in kettle and add ingredients, and boil till thick, stirring often to prevent sticking.

Put in pint jars and seal.

BOURBON PICKLE

Mrs. R. J. Neely

1 gallon of cucumbers, cut up,
1 quart of vinegar,
2 ounces of turmeric,
¼ pound of ground mustard,
6 teacups of white sugar,
2 scant cups of flour,
½ teaspoon of red pepper,
2 tablespoons of ground cinnamon,
1 tablespoon of mace,
2 ground nutmegs,
½ teacup of mustard seed,
2 tablespoons of celery seed,
1 quart of small onions,
1 head of cauliflower.

Use white spine cucumbers, and sprinkle with salt and let them lie over night. If cucumbers are in brine, soak a day and night before using.

Heat the ingredients in the 1 quart of vinegar and let the flour thicken the mixture. Add 2 quarts of vinegar, previously heated, and pour over cucumbers. Seal in stone jars; ready for use.

It is better to cook both onions and cauliflower a little before putting in vinegar with the spices.

CABBAGE PICKLE

Take enough cabbage to fill a 2-gallon jar and pour over it hot brine. Let it remain 4 days. Squeeze them out of the brine and add weak vinegar. After 3 days take strong vinegar and add

2 ounces cinnamon,
1 ounce cloves,
2 ounces turmeric,
1 ounce white mustard seed,
1 tablespoon black pepper,
2 tablespoons sugar,
1 tablespoon ginger.

Boil vinegar and spices and add cabbage, etc., and boil tender.

CAULIFLOWER PICKLE

Miss Elise White

Take the green leaves off the cauliflower and put in strong, boiling salt water and boil till tender. Dip in cold water to chill it to the heart and cut in sections. Put in jars and cover with the following: To ½ gallon of vinegar put

1 pound of sugar,
2 tablespoons of ground ginger,
2 tablespoons of English mustard seed,
2 tablespoons of turmeric, which has been mixed
    with mustard till smooth—a little cold vinegar will help it mix nicely,
1 tablespoon white mustard seed,
1 tablespoon black pepper,
1 tablespoon cinnamon,
1 tablespoon allspice.

Let this come to a boil and pour over the cauliflower, and cover tightly and let it stand for a week. Pour off the liquor, boil again, and pour over cauliflower, and bottle for use.

CHOPPED
CUCUMBER PICKLE

Mrs. B. F. Buckner

3 quarts of cucumbers,
1 quart of onions.

Soak 2 days in brine. Put in fresh water; then drain well; then boil in vinegar. Season with

1 quart of brown sugar,

5 cents' worth of turmeric,
5 cents' worth of white mustard,
5 cents' worth of celery seed,
1 teaspoon of black pepper.

Just before taking off the fire, dissolve 3 table-spoonfuls of flour in cold vinegar and put in to thicken.

CHOPPED PICKLE

Miss Mary Bashford

1 gallon of chopped tomatoes,
½ gallon of chopped cabbage,
1 quart of onions,
1 ounce of turmeric,
1 tablespoon of cloves,
4 tablespoons of ginger,
2 tablespoons of salt,
2 tablespoons of celery seed,
2 pounds or more of sugar,
3 quarts of *good* vinegar,
2 pods of green peppers.

Chop; measure each separately; boil 1 hour.

CHOW-CHOW

Mrs. Henry C. Buckner

2 heads of cauliflower,
200 very small cucumbers,
50 small onions,
1 good head of cabbage,
A few green grapes, radish pods, and nasturtium
  seeds,
½ pound of white mustard seed,
½ pound of celery seed,
¼ teacup of ground pepper,
¼ teacup of cinnamon,
½ pint of grated horseradish.

Put the cauliflower, cabbage, cucumbers, and onions in salt over night. Drain off and put to soak in vinegar 2 days. Drain again and mix with spices. Boil a gallon of vinegar with 2 pounds of sugar and pour over while hot. Do this 3 mornings in succession; then mix some ground mustard and a little olive oil until a good flavor.

DELICIOUS
CUCUMBER PICKLE

Use cucumber pickles that have been made, and slice and add pieces of chopped onions. Let the onions lie in salt water. Put in a porcelain kettle 1 quart best vinegar, made sweet with brown sugar. Color with turmeric. Season highly with allspice, cloves, cinnamon, ginger, white and black mustard seed, celery seed. Put in when boiling the cucumbers and onions and cook till pickles are a rich color. Let them cool and seal in jars.

EXCELLENT MIXED PICKLES

4 large heads of cabbage,
1 peck green tomatoes,
2 dozen cucumbers,
1 dozen onions,
1 dozen green peppers.

Chop them separately and very fine. Mix all together, and put in a layer of mixture and sprinkle with salt. Let stand all night. Then squeeze perfectly dry with the hands, and cover with cold vinegar. Let it stand 24 hours, and squeeze as before and put in jars. Take enough vinegar to cover it and add 2 pounds sugar, $\frac{1}{2}$ ounce each of cloves, cinnamon, allspice, and mace. Let it boil, cabbage and all, till tender. Put in jars and cover closely.

GREEN MANGO PICKLES

Mrs. Henry C. Buckner

After having been in brine for several weeks, soak the mangoes in cold water for 2 days; then boil in vinegar, and let them stand in that vinegar for a week. After that, take the seed from them and fill them with the following spices:

1 pound of ginger, soaked in brine a day or two, or until soft enough to slice,

1 ounce of grain black pepper,

1 ounce of mace,

1 ounce of allspice,

1 ounce of cloves,

1 ounce of turmeric,

½ pound of garlic, soaked for a day or two in brine, then dried,

1 pint of grated horseradish,

1 pint of black mustard seed,

1 pint of white mustard seed.

Bruise all the spices and mix with teacup of olive oil. To each mango add 1 teaspoonful of brown sugar. This mixture will fill 4 dozen mangoes, having chopped up some of the indifferent ones to mix with the stuffing. Tie them up and pour

over them best cider vinegar. After a month, add
3 pounds of brown sugar. Keep closely covered,
and don't eat for a year.

GREEN PICKLE

Mrs. Henry C. Buckner

Put cucumbers, beans, small ears of corn, melons,
etc., in brine strong enough to bear an egg. Let
it stand 9 days or 2 weeks. When ready to make
the pickle up, put them in kettle with grape or
cabbage leaves and small lumps of alum. Cover
with weak vinegar and simmer slowly till they are
a fine green color. Drain them on a dish.

$\frac{1}{2}$ ounce of mace,
1 ounce of cloves,
2 ounces of allspice,
1 ounce of cinnamon,
3 ounces of white mustard seed,
1 ounce of ground mustard,
2 ounces of whole grain black pepper,
1 ounce of race ginger,
1 ounce of celery seed,
$\frac{1}{2}$ pint of scraped horseradish.

Put spices in vinegar and pour boiling hot over
pickle. Tie up closely in stone jars.

GREEN SWEETMEATS

Mrs. Cyrus McCormick

1½ dozen large, green, perfectly formed cucumbers. Put them in salt and water for 3 days. Then lay them in fresh water, changing the water till all salt is extracted. Cut a slit in the side and remove the seed. Green them in vinegar and water, with a little alum. Put them in very cold water again. For the stuffing use the best raisins, citron cut in small pieces, conserved ginger and orange peel, and candied cherries. Fill each cucumber with the mixture, bring the sides together with a few stitches. Make a syrup of 1½ pounds cut loaf sugar and 1 teacup of water to each pound of cucumbers. Add green ginger, sliced, with 1 ounce of stick cinnamon and a broken nutmeg (tied in a little muslin bag and cooked in the syrup). Put the cucumbers in the syrup and cover well, and boil till clear and tender. Remove to a jar, and when the syrup is rich and thick pour over the cucumbers. Great care is required or the cucumbers may be tough. Scatter candied cherries in the jar with the mangoes.

HAYDEN SALAD

Miss Elise White

1 gallon cabbage,
1 gallon green tomatoes,
1 quart green peppers,
1 quart of onions,
5 tablespoonfuls mixed mustard,
2 tablespoonfuls ginger,
1 tablespoonful cinnamon,
1 tablespoonful cloves,
1 tablespoonful mace,
3 ounces turmeric,
1 ounce celery seed,
5 pounds sugar.

Take the seed out of the peppers and chop the onions fine. Sprinkle salt on tomatoes and let stand awhile; strain off the juice and throw away. Add to the cabbage, etc., the spices named. Mix well with strong vinegar and boil till done.

KENTUCKY CHOW-CHOW

2 dozen cucumbers, large,
2 cabbage heads of medium size,
½ peck of green tomatoes,

6 large onions,

18 little ears of corn, 2 or 5 inches long,

1 large head of cauliflower,

3 or 4 peppers,

3 pounds brown sugar,

½ ounce turmeric,

2 ounces white mustard seed,

2 ounces celery seed,

½ gallon vinegar.

Chop and boil the vegetables in vinegar till they are tender. Throw away this vinegar. Take 1 gallon of fresh vinegar and add the seasoning, spices, etc.

Pour over the pickles and boil 5 minutes, or till tender. Seal in stone jars.

MRS. BRENT'S
YELLOW PICKLE

After bleaching and drying the cabbage, beans, young cucumbers, small green tomatoes, peppers, etc., put them in tepid water from 6 to 12 hours. Wash them well out of this water, squeezing each handful pretty dry, and casting them into fresh cold water. Wash them several times in the cold water, allowing them to remain in this 10 or 12 hours before squeezing dry, and putting them on a dish to drain 2 or 3 hours. Then put them in a jar of light-colored cider or wine vinegar. After a week or 10 days you must change to strong vinegar, allowing $\frac{1}{2}$ ounce of turmeric to each gallon of vinegar.

Pack the cabbage and other ingredients as tight as you please, so they are kept covered by the vinegar. Sprinkle the turmeric in layers as you pack, and pour the vinegar on last. Put a weight on the pickles, so as to keep them under the vinegar. After 3 weeks divide the ingredients and put in a large jar, sprinkling the yellow mixture in layers. One small box of Lexington mustard, half the quantity of ground ginger, $\frac{1}{4}$ pint of white mustard seed, washed well first in water and then in vinegar; $1\frac{1}{2}$ dozen pieces of ginger root, 2 ounces of cinnamon, broken small; 1 tablespoonful of mace, broken in little pieces; 3 tablespoons of sugar, 1 ounce of long pepper, $1\frac{1}{2}$ ounces of turmeric. Pour on 2 gallons of strong white cider or wine vinegar; then 10 or 12 drops of oil of cloves, 1 gill of olive oil. Tie 4 or 5 cloves of garlic in muslin and lay on top.

If there is not sufficient of any flavor after a month, add the ingredient necessary.

In bleaching the peppers necessary for the pickle, keep it separate and add 5 or 6 at a time, until you think there is enough.

YELLOW PICKLE

Miss Elise White

Take cabbage, cauliflower, nasturtium seed, asparagus, tender corn, and beans. Put into a kettle and pour over them boiling salt water and let stand 24 hours. Make this pickle on a clear day, and press the water from each piece and lay to dry on a cloth in the hot sun. The cloth absorbs the moisture and the sun bleaches. By turning them often they become white and receive the turmeric better. One day of hot sun is enough to prepare them for the first vinegar. When dry, put in a jar and cover with cold plain vinegar, with a little turmeric. Let stand 2 weeks and add spiced vinegar. Mix the turmeric smoothly before adding to the vinegar.

OIL MANGOES

Mrs. Henry C. Buckner

¼ pound of garlic,
1 pound of scraped horseradish,
1 pound of white mustard seed,
1 pound of black mustard seed,
1 pint little white onions,
1 ounce of long peppers,
2 ounces of black pepper,

2 ounces of allspice,
2 ounces of turmeric,
1 ounce of mace,
1 ounce of cloves,
¼ ounce of ginger, cut up fine,
4 ounces of olive oil.

Scald the mangoes when stuffed in well-spiced vinegar.

ONION PICKLE

2 gallons small white onions,
1 pint salt.

Pour on boiling water and let stand 24 hours. Then boil in sweet milk and water until coddled. Soak a day or two in weak vinegar. Heat enough vinegar to cover and add spices (except allspice, which will make onions dark), and pour over the pickle.

PEPPER MANGOES

Put the peppers in strong brine for 2 weeks; then put in fresh water till free from salt. For 40 mangoes make a stuffing of

1 pound dried cabbage,
Grated onions, horseradish, ginger, mustard, ½
    pound each,
Mace, cinnamon, cloves, 1 ounce each.

Sew each pepper and put in a jar. Pour strong vinegar over. The cabbage must be dried and chopped fine. The horseradish dried and scraped well. All ingredients, except cabbage, to be pounded fine. Mix with olive oil or fresh butter.

PICKLED WALNUTS

After scraping walnuts, let them stand in salt water for 2 or 3 weeks. Scald twice quickly, so as not to soften them, and rub dry and put in jars. Pour boiling vinegar over them and let them stand 2 weeks longer. Then boil in very strong vinegar to every hundred walnuts 3 ounces each of mace, allspice, cloves, pepper, ginger, garlic, horseradish, and pour over walnuts and seal tightly.

PLAIN CUCUMBER PICKLE

Mrs. R. J. Neely

After washing the brine from cucumbers, place in a jar and fill almost to the top with cold vinegar. Put in a kettle

 1 quart of vinegar,
 1 pound of sugar,
 1 handful of whole black pepper,
 A few cloves,

1 or 2 pods of red pepper,
A little mace.

Boil till strength of spices is extracted; then pour over pickle. Tie securely to keep strength in. This amount is for 1 gallon of pickle.

ROUGH-AND-READY PICKLE

3 dozen cucumbers,
½ peck green tomatoes,
½ dozen peppers,
½ dozen onions.

Salt them separately and let stand over night. Then press till perfectly dry. The peppers and onions chopped fine. Take enough vinegar to cover, and add

2 tablespoons black pepper,
2 tablespoons allspice,
3 tablespoons white mustard seed,
3 tablespoons celery seed,
1 tablespoon horseradish,
½ dozen cloves.

Let it come to a boil and then add cabbage, etc. Put in jar and seal.

SLICED CUCUMBER PICKLE

E. D. P.

Peel and slice separately. Sprinkle well with salt, and let them stand over night. Squeeze them through a cloth.

To 4 pounds of cucumbers, add
- 2 pounds of sliced onions,
- 2 quarts of vinegar,
- 1 pound of brown sugar,
- 8 green peppers, cut in small pieces,
- 2 tablespoons of celery seed,
- 2 tablespoons of turmeric,
- 6 tablespoons of white mustard seed,
- 2 tablespoons of grated horseradish.

Put all on fire and let it come to a good boil. When cold, add 3 tablespoonfuls of olive oil.

SPANISH PICKLE (No. 1)

Mrs. Henry C. Buckner

- 2 dozen cucumbers,
- $\frac{1}{2}$ peck of green tomatoes,
- 2 large green peppers, seeds taken out,
- 2 dozen white onions, sliced,
- $\frac{1}{2}$ peck of beans.

Slice cucumbers thick, tomatoes thin, and sprinkle them with salt. Let stand 24 hours. Wash off the salt and let them drain well.

1 pint of grated horseradish,
1 pound of white mustard seed,
5 long red peppers,
15 cents' worth of cinnamon.

Make a paste of

1 pound of mustard (Colman's),
2 ounces of turmeric,
2 ounces of celery seed,
1 pint bottle of olive oil,
4 teacups of brown sugar,
1 handful of garlic.

Put vegetables in a large pan, mix spices and paste well together, and pour boiling vinegar over all—enough to cover well. Very fine.

In place of tomatoes and beans, use cauliflower and celery.

SPANISH PICKLE (No. 2)
Mrs. H. C. McDowell

½ peck of cucumbers out of the brine,
½ peck of small green beans and tomatoes together,

2 dozen small onions, scalded twice in boiling salt
water,

Slice and salt tomatoes over night, drain well next
day,

Slice the cucumbers lengthwise,

Take 1 box mustard seed,

2 ounces turmeric and mix well with 4 tablespoons
of olive oil and put in bottom of jar.

Have ready 1 ounce cinnamon,

2 ounces celery seed,

½ pound white mustard seed,

2 roots horseradish sliced.

Slice the tomatoes and cut onions in half.
Put in layers of spices and vegetables alternately in the jar, pour over hot vinegar, allowing
1½ pounds sugar to a gallon of vinegar or more,
if desired. Stir well from bottom every day for a
week, and it will then be ready for use.

SPICED VINEGAR

Miss Elise White

½ pound ginger,

¼ pound garlic,

½ pound horseradish,

½ pound white pepper,

$\frac{1}{4}$ pound cinnamon,

3 ounces turmeric,

$\frac{1}{2}$ ounce allspice,

$\frac{1}{2}$ ounce mace,

$\frac{1}{2}$ ounce cloves.

Put in jar with 1 gallon of good vinegar. Prepare this some time before it is used.

STUFFING FOR MELONS
E. D. P.

$\frac{1}{2}$ pound of ground race ginger,

1 pound of scraped horseradish,

1 pound of white mustard seed,

1 pound of chopped onion,

1 ounce of ground mace,

1 ounce of grated nutmeg,

$\frac{1}{2}$ cup of black pepper grains,

1 tablespoon of celery seed,

$\frac{1}{4}$ pound of ground mustard,

2 ounces of turmeric.

Make into a paste with 1 pint of best salad oil. Fill each melon, putting in each a small clove of garlic. Seal tightly and pack in a jar and put a little stuffing over each layer; also a piece of alum the size of a hickory nut, and kept well covered with cider vinegar.

317

SWEET PEACH PICKLE

Peel 1 gallon of cling-stone peaches.
Boil ½ gallon·vinegar with ½ pound sugar. Add
    spices to taste.

Spices must be tied in a bag. Pour over peaches
and put aside over night. Then pour off and boil
and again pour over the fruit. Do this nine mornings, and the last time put fruit in syrup and boil
till tender. Put in jar and cover tightly. Can be
used at any time.

SWEET PICKLE

7 pounds fruit, cherries, damsons, peaches, or any
    kind of fruit,
3 pounds sugar,
1 quart cider vinegar,
1 ounce cinnamon,
½ ounce cloves,
Ginger and mace to taste.

Pour over fruit. For two mornings, vinegar and
spices must be boiled and poured over the fruit.
The third morning put all in kettle and simmer a
few minutes. Tie closely and keep in a dark closet.

WATERMELON PICKLE

Prepare the rind by paring the outside and using only the firm part of the melon, cut in shapes, and let it lie over night in weak alum water. Soak in clear water one day.

To 5 pounds fruit take $\frac{1}{2}$ the amount of sugar, 1 quart of vinegar, and boil. Add slices of 1 lemon and spices to taste, cinnamon, ginger, mace. Pour hot over the fruit and let stand over night. Pour off and boil, and do this three mornings, the last time putting the fruit in the syrup, and cook till it can be pierced with a fork. Put in jars and seal.

Catsups

___

CABBAGE CATSUP

Chop very fine

> 4 heads of cabbage,
> 4 large onions,
> 3 green peppers,
> 1 dozen cucumbers.

Sprinkle with salt and put in bag and hang up to drain over night. Add to the vinegar, which must be enough to cover cabbage, etc.:

> $\frac{1}{2}$ pound white mustard seed,
> 2   tablespoons made mustard,
> 1   tablespoon cinnamon,
> 1   tablespoon allspice,
> 1   tablespoon mace,
> 2   tablespoons celery seed,
> 2   tablespoons ground pepper,

12 tablespoons turmeric,
2 teacups brown sugar.

Boil and then add cabbage, etc., and boil till tender. Bottle while hot.

CHILI SAUCE

3 small green or red peppers,
12 tomatoes,
3 large onions,
2 tablespoons salt,
3 tablespoons sugar,
1 tablespoon cinnamon,
1 tablespoon black pepper,
3 cups vinegar,
1 tablespoon made mustard,
1 tablespoon mustard seed,
1 tablespoon mace,
1 grated nutmeg.

Peel tomatoes and onions and slice fine. Chop the peppers and add altogether with the other ingredients and boil till thick, about 2 hours. This is a good recipe, and will keep a long time if put in bottles and tightly corked. It may be made in the winter when ripe tomatoes can not be had by using 2 quarts of canned tomatoes in the place of the 12 ripe ones.

CUCUMBER CATSUP (No. 1)

Miss Elise White

- 3 good cucumbers,
- 3 onions,
- ½ pint salt,
- 1 wineglass pepper (black),
- 1 wineglass white mustard,
- 1 wineglass black mustard.

Chop up onions and cucumbers fine, mix together, sprinkle with salt and let stand 24 hours on a dish in the sun, if possible; add other ingredients and cover with strong vinegar. Bottle and seal.

CUCUMBER CATSUP (No. 2)

Mrs. Simms

To 1 peck of large cucumbers, peeled and seeds all removed, and grated or ground, take 1 dozen onions, also grated. Over these pour salt and water, and let stand 24 hours. Make the water just salty enough to taste good, not *brine*. Do not mix the onions with the cucumbers until after they have dripped the last time. Pour the ground vegetables in bags and hang up until they are well drained. Then put in a jar and pour weak vinegar and alum over, and let stand 2 days. Drip again until dry, mix the vegetables and white mustard seed in jar, and pour over strong, good vinegar in which you have boiled sugar and turmeric. Use 2 pints of good brown sugar to 1 gallon of strong vinegar and 2 tablespoons of turmeric. Put in stone jar for about 2 weeks and then seal in quart jars.

MUSHROOM CATSUP

Gather fresh mushrooms and put alternate layers of salt and mushrooms in a jar and let them stand 24 hours. Stir them up and let them stand 2 days. Strain and put on the stove and let it boil.

To 1 quart of liquor add
1 ounce allspice,
1 ounce ginger,
2 teaspoons cayenne pepper,
1 teaspoon mace,
1 teaspoon cloves.

Boil till thick. While catsup is hot, bottle and seal. Nice for soups.

RIPE TOMATO CATSUP

Mrs. John W. Fox

1 peck ripe tomatoes,
4 onions,

1 quart cider vinegar,

3 green peppers, or 1 spoon of cayenne,

3 cups brown sugar,

4 pieces of ginger or 2 tablespoons ground ginger,

3 tablespoons salt,

2 tablespoons black pepper,

2 tablespoons made mustard,

2 tablespoons cloves,

2 tablespoons celery seed,

2 tablespoons cinnamon,

2 tablespoons allspice,

2 tablespoons white mustard seed.

Prepare the tomatoes and cut up with the onions and boil in their own liquid till tender. Let them cool, then strain through colander and add spices, sugar, and vinegar and let them boil 2½ hours or till very thick. Bottle and seal while hot.

TOMATO CATSUP

½ bushel of tomatoes,

½ pound of salt,

2 pounds of brown sugar,

1 ounce of allspice,

½ ounce of cayenne pepper,

6 large onions,

1 quart of vinegar,
2 nutmegs added when the mixture is done.

Boil till thick.

WALNUT CATSUP

Put the walnuts in salt for a week.

Crush in a mortar and cover with hot vinegar and let stand a week.

Strain through a colander and allow for each quart:

½ ounce black pepper,
1 ounce ginger,
½ ounce cloves,
1 nutmeg,
1 teaspoon celery seed tied in a bag,
1 teaspoon allspice,
1 pinch cayenne pepper and boil for 2 hours.
Bottle while hot.

Preserves

APPLE MARMALADE

¾ pound sugar to 1 pound of fruit.

Use tart apples. Add water and cook to a thick pulp. Measure and add ¾ pound of sugar to 1 pound fruit. Stir well all the time to keep from burning, and remove the scum as it rises. Flavor with cinnamon and lemon to taste. Put in stone jars and cover well.

BLACKBERRY JAM (No. 1)

Wash and pick the berries and mash well with the hands. Be sure to squeeze out the heart, which is very hard. Weigh the fruit and put ¾ pound sugar to 1 pound fruit. Boil in a porcelain kettle. ·Remove scum as it rises and stir constantly to prevent sticking at bottom. Let it cook till thick.

BLACKBERRY JAM (No. 2)

Use recipe above, but strain through a colander and remove the seed before cooking. This makes a clear jam, and many people prefer it.

DELICIOUS APPLE PRESERVES

Mrs. J. W. Fox

If sour apples are used, take 1 pound sugar to 1 pound fruit.

If sweet apples are used, take ¾ pound of sugar to 1 pound fruit.

Make a rich syrup of sugar and water and boil till thick. Slice ½ lemon and drop in syrup. Pare and core the apples and drop them whole in the syrup a few at a time and cook till they can be pierced with a fork. Remove fruit and put in glass jar, and drop more apples in the syrup. Boil the syrup that is left till quite thick and fill the jars.

FRANKFORD PRESERVED ORANGES

Mrs. Francis McCormick

Remove the outside skin as thin as possible with a sharp knife and boil the oranges in water till they can be pierced with a straw. Make a small hole and take out each seed with the handle of a teaspoon. Add sugar to the water—2 pounds of sugar to 1 pound of fruit—and skim before putting the oranges in. Boil till clear.

GINGER PEARS

Mrs. Simms

Ginger pears are a delicious sweetmeat. Use hard pears. Peel, core, and cut the fruit into very thin slices. For 8 pounds of fruit, after it has been sliced, use the same quantity of sugar, the juice of 4 lemons, 1 pint of water, and ½ pound of ginger root sliced thin. Cut the lemon rinds into as long and thin strips as possible. Place all together in a preserving kettle and boil slowly for an hour.

ORANGE MARMALADE

E. D. P.

Remove the rind and seeds from the oranges.
Cut the rind of $\frac{1}{2}$ in fine strips and parboil in water
till enough of the bitter has been removed and
sufficient taste remains to flavor the pulp nicely.
Cut up the pulp as fine as possible and mix with the
rind. To every pound of fruit add 1 pound of
granulated sugar.

Put into a preserving kettle and stir slowly all
the time it is boiling. When it is a clear golden
color, it is done.

This is delicious with ice cream, plain cream, or
on pastry puffs.

PEACH CONSERVES

Mrs. Cyrus McCormick

Pare, quarter, and remove the stones from yellow cling peaches.

To every 4 pounds of fruit make a syrup of 1
pound of cut loaf sugar and $\frac{1}{2}$ teacup of water.
Drop the peaches in, a few at a time, and boil till
clear and tender. Spread on large dishes and
drain off all juice. Sprinkle with granulated sugar

and set them in the sun to dry for 3 days, each day turning them and sprinkling with sugar. When they are sufficiently candied pack in glass jars with dry sugar.

PEACH PRESERVES

1 pound sugar to 1 pound fruit.

Peel, stone, and halve peaches. Add enough water to the sugar to make a thick syrup, and boil till thick. Put in fruit and cook till clear and tender. A few stones added make a delicious flavor. Use firm peaches, as over-ripe ones lose their form and the under-ripe ones make dark preserves.

PEAR PRESERVES

V. C. G.

8 pounds of pears, nearly ripe,
8 pounds of sugar,
4 lemons, peel very fine, and squeeze the juice,
$\frac{1}{4}$ pound of green ginger,
1 tumbler of water.

Put all in a kettle together, and let boil $\frac{3}{4}$ of an hour, or until the syrup is the right consistency.

RIPE TOMATO PRESERVES VERY FINE

Mrs. John W. Fox

7 pounds ripe tomatoes,
7 pounds sugar.

Put the sugar on the fruit and let stand over night. Drain off syrup, which boil and skim well. Put in tomatoes and boil gently 20 minutes. Take the fruit out and spread on a dish. Boil the syrup till it thickens. Flavor with ginger and cinnamon. Put the fruit in the syrup and cook 10 minutes. Put in jars, which are in hot water. Seal or tie up closely.

GREEN TOMATO PRESERVES

Use same recipe as above except season with ginger and mace. Cover at once.

SPICED PEACHES

1 peck of peeled peaches,
$3\frac{1}{2}$ pounds of brown sugar,
3 pints of cider vinegar,
$\frac{1}{2}$ ounce of nutmeg,
1 ounce of cloves,
1 ounce of cinnamon.

Peel the peaches and put in a stone jar. Break up spices and strew them through the peaches. Boil sugar and vinegar together 10 minutes, and pour on the peaches while very hot. Repeat this for 3 consecutive days, then boil all together for 10 minutes.

Plums can be done the same way—adding less vinegar.

SPICED PLUMS
V. C. G.

6 pounds of damsons,
4 pounds of coffee sugar,
1 pint of vinegar.

Boil to a thick jam, taking out the stones as they rise to the top. Just before taking off the jam stir in

2 tablespoons of powdered cloves,
2 tablespoons of powdered cinnamon.

This is nice to serve with cold meats. The damsons should be thoroughly ripe.

STRAWBERRY PRESERVES

1 pound fruit to ¾ pound of sugar.

Boil sugar and water till a clear thick syrup. Drop the berries and cook till clear and thick. Pour in jars and seal.

Jellies

APPLE JELLY

Mrs. John W. Fox

Put apples which have been quartered into granite kettle, and cover with 1 pint water to 1 gallon of fruit. Boil till fruit is soft. Strain and add 2 pints sugar to 3 pints juice and boil rapidly, taking all scum off. When it begins to jelly, pour into glasses and cover with brandied paper.

BLACKBERRY JELLY

Miss Mary Bashford

To 1 quart of juice,
Add 2 pints of water.
To 4 pints of juice,
Add 3 pints of sugar.

CRABAPPLE JELLY

Cut the apples into quarters and cover with water and boil till tender. Strain through a flannel bag and add 1 pint sugar to 1 pint juice. Boil juice 20 minutes, at the same time melt the sugar in a kettle. Pour together and boil till it begins to jelly. Skim constantly. Fill glasses and set in dark closet.

CURRANT JELLY

Pick stems from currants and put in stone jar in kettle of boiling water and cook till skins break. Do not put water over them. Strain through a flannel bag and add 1 pint sugar to each pint juice. Boil the juice while the sugar melts and pour together and boil till it begins to jelly. Strain again and pour in glasses, which must be in hot water.

GRAPE JELLY

Pick stems from grapes. Put in jar without water and set in kettle of hot water and cook till fruit bursts. Strain in flannel bag and to 1 pint juice add 1 pint sugar. Boil till it begins to jelly and pour in glasses. Cover with paper which has been dipped in brandy, which prevents mould, and set aside in dark place.

WILD PLUM JELLY

Mrs. J. W. Fox

To 1 gallon of plums add 1 quart water. Let boil till tender, then strain and add to each pint of juice 1 pint sugar. Let juice boil while the sugar melts in a kettle or pan. Pour together and boil till it begins to jelly. Test it by taking a teaspoonful and let it cool. Pour into jelly glasses and set aside to cool. Care must be taken that it does not boil too long. This makes a beautiful jelly.

Confections

BROWN TAFFY

3 pounds sugar,
½ pound butter,
1 teaspoon cream of tartar.

Put in pan and dissolve with water. Boil till it cracks. Flavor with vanilla. Pour on marble slab and when cool enough to pull, pull till light, and arrange in long strips and cut any length desired.

CARAMEL CANDY

¼ pound chocolate,
1 pound brown sugar,
1 cup of sweet cream,
1 tablespoon of butter.

Boil till thick and flavor with vanilla. Beat till creamy. Pour on slab and cut in squares.

CHOCOLATE CANDY

3 cups white sugar,
2 tablespoons butter,
1 tablespoon vinegar and $\frac{1}{4}$ teaspoon soda,
$\frac{1}{4}$ cake of chocolate,
1 cup of boiling water.

Put all in a pan and stir till dissolved, boil till it cracks, flavor with vanilla, and beat till creamy. Pour on slab and cut in squares.

CHOCOLATE CARAMELS

To 1 pint of rich milk, add

3 pounds of light-brown sugar,
$\frac{1}{2}$ pound of butter.

Let the mixture come to a boil, when add $\frac{1}{2}$ pound of scraped chocolate. Let it boil till it becomes quite thick, stirring it all the time. It is best to mix the chocolate with a cup of the boiling milk before adding it to the whole.

When done, flavor with vanilla; pour into buttered pans, and cut in squares before it becomes quite cold.

CHOCOLATE DROPS

Miss Kate Alexander

2 pounds of powdered sugar,
Whites of 2 eggs,
⅓ cup of sugar,
1 tablespoonful of vanilla,
1½ pounds of grated pecans.

Beat the whites of 2 eggs. Sift the sugar; then pour gradually into the eggs, stirring rapidly. Put in the vanilla; then the grated nuts; then pour in the cream. Add the rest of the sugar until it can be worked as dough; then roll out in any shape, and put on a dish to cool.

Take ¾ cake of chocolate (melted); then drop them in, taking out with a toothpick on either side. Place them on buttered paper; then put a pecan on top. Set out to cool; then put them on a dish.

COCOANUT CANDY

1 cocoanut, grated,
3 cups brown sugar.

Cover the sugar with water and cook till brittle. Then pour over the cocoanut, which has been sprinkled on either slab or dish.

When cold, break in small pieces.

COCOANUT FUDGE

Miss Kate Alexander

3 cups of light-brown sugar,
Enough cream to mix well,
1 pinch of salt,
1 pinch of soda,
1 teaspoonful of vanilla,
Butter size of a hen's egg,
1 box of cocoanut.

Mix the sugar well with cream; then cook till it boils. Add the soda and salt. Later, put in the butter and cocoanut; add the vanilla just before taking off. Take off before quite done, beat until stiff, and pour into a dish.

CREAM CANDY

3 pounds sugar,
1 pint cream,
1 cup water,
2 tablespoons vinegar and $\frac{1}{2}$ teaspoon soda,
1 tablespoon butter.

Boil till it cracks against the side of a glass, and pour on slab. Flavor to taste, and pull with the fingers till light.

EGG KISSES

Whites of 3 eggs,
1 pint sugar.

Put the sugar in a bowl and pour the whites over and beat 20 minutes. With a dessertspoon drop the mixture on paper an inch or more apart. Do not let them touch. Put on a board or an inverted bread-pan, and put enough layers of paper to keep the bottom from burning. Bake in a moderate oven till brown. Let the mixture rise and then bake, or they will not be light. Remove with a knife and put on a dish.

CHOCOLATE EGG KISSES

Follow preceding recipe, and add before cooking 1 ounce grated chocolate, which has been melted. Add gently and quickly, or the mixture will be too thin. Bake according to above directions.

343

FONDANT

Miss Mary Bashford

1 pound of sugar,
1 saltspoon of cream of tartar,
1 teacup of cold water.

Stir all together, and boil till it forms a jelly-like consistency when tried in cold water. When done, take from stove and let stand 10 minutes. Then beat well till a creamy mass.

This fondant is the foundation for a variety of candies.

FUDGE

Miss Kate Alexander

3 cups of brown sugar,
Just enough cream to wet the sugar,
1 pinch of salt,
1 pinch of soda,
1 teaspoonful of vanilla,
Butter size of a hen's egg,
⅓ cake of chocolate.

Stir the cream well into the sugar; then place it on the stove. Watch carefully, so it cannot burn; then, when it begins to boil, add salt and soda. Later, put in the chocolate and butter. Take it

344

off before it is quite done; then add the vanilla. Beat it until it creams; then pour in a dish. Put out to cool and cut in squares.

NAN'S CANDY

2 pints of light-brown sugar wet with cream.

Don't cook too much. When it begins to boil, put in a good-sized lump of butter.

After taking it off, put in vanilla, stir hard, and add nuts.

PEANUT BRITTLE

1 pint brown sugar,
1 pint shelled peanuts.

Melt the sugar in a pan till it boils and turns color; then pour over the nuts, which have been scattered on a well-buttered slab.

Cut in squares or break in pieces.

PEPPERMINT CANDY

2 teacups white sugar,
1 tablespoon butter,
1 tablespoon vinegar and $\frac{1}{4}$ teaspoon soda,
$\frac{1}{2}$ cup of boiling water.

Set on stove and stir till thoroughly dissolved.

Cook till brittle. Remove from the stove, flavor with 3 or 4 drops of oil of peppermint, and beat till creamy. Pour on slab and cut in squares.

PRALINES

Mrs. Tom R. Wyles

(A Creole Recipe)

Equal quantity of nuts and sugar.

Use brown sugar, not too light or too dark, but medium.

Moisten the sugar with cream and heat it; then add 1 tablespoon vinegar, and boil a few minutes. Add the nuts and beat till it sugars.

SALTED ALMONDS

Take any quantity of almonds and blanch them, being careful to dry them thoroughly. Put in a baking-pan, let them heat well, and add a little fresh butter or olive oil. Sprinkle with salt and toast a delicate brown.

WHITE CREAM CANDY

4 pounds white sugar,
1 teaspoon cream of tartar.

Enough water to cover. Put the sugar in a

pan and add the cream of tartar. Cover with water. When it cracks, flavor and pour on buttered slab and pull with fingers till light. Cut in lengths desired.

WHITE TAFFY CANDY

3 pounds sugar,
½ pound butter,
1 teaspoon cream of tartar.

Boil till it cracks and pour on slab. Flavor and pull till white.

Cheese

CHEESE OMELET

Mrs. H. C. McDowell

Stir 1 teacup of bread-crumbs into 1 pint of
scalded milk. Add butter the size of an egg, a
little salt, and ½ cup grated cheese. Then add 3
eggs beaten separately. Bake 15 or 20 minutes
in a hot oven.

CHEESE SOUFFLÉ

Mrs. Henry C. Buckner

½ pound of cheese, grated,
3 eggs,
1 cup of milk,
2 even tablespoons of butter,
1 heaping tablespoon of flour,
½ teaspoon of salt.

Make a sauce of the butter, flour, and milk.

Add the cheese and salt; lastly, the yolks of the eggs, well beaten.

When cold, and just before baking, add the well-beaten whites; put into small buttered shells, and place in shallow pans with water. Bake 20 minutes.

CHEESE STICKS

Make the finest pastry—1 pound of flour makes a good-sized dish. Roll the pastry about $\frac{1}{3}$ or $\frac{1}{2}$ inch thick. Cut accurately in sticks 5 inches long and $\frac{2}{3}$ of an inch wide. Sprinkle heavily with finely grated cheese and bake a light brown.

CHEESE STRAWS

Mrs. Henry C. Buckner

8 tablespoons of flour,
8 tablespoons of grated cheese,
4 tablespoons of butter,
1 teaspoon of baking-powder,
1 egg,
Pinch of cayenne pepper and salt.

Roll *very thin* and cut into straws.